Pevsner Introductions

Churches
AN ARCHITECTURAL GUIDE

Simon Bradley

Yale University Press | New Haven and London

Pevsner Introductions draw extensively on the Pevsner Architectural Guides, the series founded by Sir Nikolaus Pevsner in 1951. Readers wishing to know more about the architecture of a particular area should consult the relevant **Buildings of England** volume. There are also companion series for the **Buildings of Ireland**, **Scotland** and **Wales**. Specialist terms given in small capitals in this text are explained in more detail in *Pevsner's Architectural Glossary*, available both in print and as an app.

YALE UNIVERSITY PRESS | NEW HAVEN AND LONDON
www.pevsner.co.uk   www.yalebooks.co.uk
www.lookingatbuildings.com   www.yalebooks.com

© Yale University 2016
This paperback edition published 2017
10 9 8 7 6 5 4 3 2 1

Designed by Catherine Bankhurst
Typeset in Johnston ITC Standard and Minion Pro
Printed in China

British Library Cataloguing in Publication Data
Data available
Library of Congress Cataloging in Publication Data
Data available

ISBN 9780300233438

Frontispiece: All Saints, Selsley, Gloucestershire, by G. F. Bodley, 1860–2
Endpapers: Selected church plans from the Pevsner Architectural Guides

Contents

INTRODUCTION

Whatever their beliefs, most people living in England will find themselves at one time or another inside an Anglican parish church, or just looking curiously at one from outside. This book is for anyone who wants to know more about these buildings, both architecturally and in terms of how they have been furnished and used over the centuries.

There are currently about 16,000 such churches – that is to say, the parish buildings of the Church of England, in its home territory. Some 8,500 are thought to include at least some medieval fabric, and a great many of these are wholly medieval or very nearly so. Of the rest, most belong to the great church-building years of the C19 and early C20, especially the Victorian decades. In 1841, the Church of England owned 12,668 places of parish worship; in 1876, 15,867; in 1901, 18,026. The gap between that figure and the modern total is a sign of how many churches have fallen victim to war damage, declining attendance or demographic change.

An English parish church, reduced to its bare outlines on a greetings card or in a cartoon, will follow a familiar pattern. It will have a tower at one end, with or without a spire. Its windows will have pointed, that is to say Gothic, arches. As for the setting, it will usually be shown in its own churchyard, perhaps with an attendant tree or two.

Of course, many churches do not match this outline at all. Georgian and Modernist examples in particular have their own distinctive character, often radically unlike any native medieval type. Some urban churches may be hemmed in on all sides, their form determined by the space available. Recent buildings may combine

▲ 2. A typical English village church: St John the Baptist, Tunstall, Lancashire, built mostly in the C15

uses or share ownership with other congregations in ways that would leave the churchgoers of earlier generations dumbfounded. Yet a very high proportion of Anglican buildings – especially those with medieval origins, and Victorian churches that follow the Gothic style – do fit the popular stereotype.

What follows focuses on the architecture and furnishings of England's purpose-built parish churches of all periods and styles. It does not include the great cathedrals, or the eighty-plus monastic church complexes that have survived in various states of preservation for use by Anglican parishes. Nor does it cover churchyards and settings, or the chapels at colleges, schools, barracks, cemeteries, hospitals, and wherever else the Established Church has sought to provide places of worship, still less the distinctive inheritances of religious architecture in Wales, Scotland and Ireland. England's diverse and relatively tolerant religious history has also produced a mass of buildings for different denominations – from spectacular Roman Catholic cathedrals to the plain and self-effacing meeting houses of the Quakers (Society of Friends), not to mention places of worship of non-Christian faiths. It would be impossible to embrace so much variety in a book of this size without an excess of hurry and skimming.

Instead, the chapters explore the ways in which the parish churches of England have developed through the centuries. These changes sometimes correspond to shifts in religious ideas and practices, or to wider architectural fashions, or both. Interspersed with the chronological chapters are features on the fittings, furnishings and monuments that are an inseparable part of the appeal of church visiting.

The book draws on twenty years' work for the Pevsner Architectural Guides, including first-hand surveys of hundreds of churches in city, town and country. It can be read independently, or as a complement to the *Buildings of England* series which Sir Nikolaus Pevsner founded in 1951. Authors who write for the series must look closely at each church building, inside and out, contents included. They must compare published accounts with the physical reality, staying alert for clues that may have been missed. Every visit is at once a problem-solving mission and a potential treasure hunt. Was the church built in a single campaign, or is it a composite of more than one period? Which features look earlier or later than one another, and what might this imply about how the fabric evolved? Does the building show the influence of a cathedral, abbey or other great church? Are those windows or that piece of carving original, or Victorian restoration? What are the furnishings, stained glass and monuments like, and do their forms or inscriptions shed their own light on the church's story? Besides its historic and architectural interest, what are the visual pleasures that the church has to offer? Once the visit is over, what lingers most in the mind's eye and imagination?

Expert or beginner, resident or visitor, anyone can join in a similar quest. A little knowledge goes a long way – and if this book helps to increase the understanding and enjoyment of looking at churches, it will have served its purpose.

Christianity was established in Britain before the end of Roman rule in the c5, but it was disrupted by the pagan Anglo-Saxon invasions that followed, so that any continuity is hard to trace. It took two separate missionary movements, one from the independent Celtic church of Ireland and the other from papal Rome, to renew the Christian culture of England. Each mission had its own architectural traditions, and although their physical legacy is modest, the few remaining early Anglo-Saxon churches are powerfully resonant buildings.

The churches of the Roman mission, begun by St Augustine of Canterbury in 598, were mostly placed in former Roman sites – towns and forts – in present-day Kent and Essex. A political point was made here, for the popes of the Roman church claimed authority over that of the Celts. The best-preserved example is at Bradwell-on-Sea in Essex, built probably in the mid c7. It is a simple rectangle

▲ 3. St Peter-on-the-Wall, Bradwell-on-Sea, Essex. An early Anglo-Saxon church built c. 654 of salvaged Roman materials, now reduced to the nave only

▲ 4. All Saints, Brixworth, Northants, nave interior, looking W. The late C8 or C9 side walls have blocked arches made of reused Roman bricks, each formerly opening to a separate chamber known as a *porticus*. Later in Anglo-Saxon times a full tower was added in place of the original W attachment, with a triple-arched window looking into the nave

in plan, but formerly had a rounded APSE for the altar projecting from the E end; this was separated by a triple ARCADE or screen of columns from the main space, or NAVE. On each side of the nave and entered from it was a subsidiary room known as a PORTICUS; these were probably used as burial chapels. The apse-ended form derived from the BASILICAS of the Romans, which were public buildings used as courtrooms and for other assemblies. The early Church is thought to have adopted the form as a way of distinguishing its buildings from pagan temples.

Some of these features recur in the late C7 and C8 churches of Northumbria, which was evangelised by both Roman and Celtic missionaries from the 620s onwards. Escomb in County Durham is the least altered survivor. The chief difference is in the overall proportions, which are longer, narrower and higher than those of the southern churches – and even these are generally taller than those of the Norman churches that came afterwards. At Escomb, these proportions extend to the simple arch in the cross-wall which divides the nave from the

ANGLO-SAXON 11

CHANCEL, where the altar stands. The chancel almost always represented the more sacred space within the church, and was reserved for the priest; the nave was for the congregation. At Escomb the chancel is oblong in plan with a straight E wall instead of an apse in the Roman manner. On the other hand, the use of salvaged Roman masonry to build Escomb, Jarrow and other churches of the period is another assertion of continuity with the greater Church beyond English shores.

Roman material – thin bricks, rather than stone – was also used at the largest surviving Anglo-Saxon church, at Brixworth in Northamptonshire. As constructed in the late C8 or C9, this enigmatic building had rows of *porticus* on both sides of the nave and

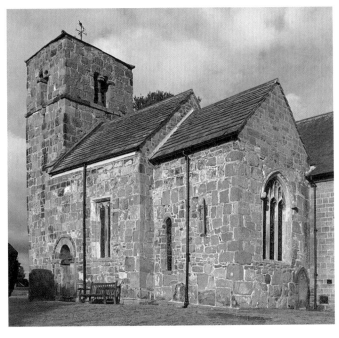

5. St John, Kirk Hammerton, North Yorkshire (formerly West Riding). An Anglo-Saxon church of uncertain date, extended to the N in the C19. The simply ornamented S doorway and twin belfry opening are typically Anglo-Saxon, and the nave and chancel show the tall and narrow proportions favoured in Northumbria

part-way alongside the chancel. The demolition of the *porticus* later in the Middle Ages has exposed their blocked entrance arches on the outer walls, below the round-arched windows of the CLERESTORY that light the nave from high up in its walls. Large churches of this kind were known as MINSTERS, and were the headquarters of groups of priests who served the surrounding region; the term may survive as a place-name suffix, long after the Anglo-Saxon building was replaced.

A few churches of the period are faced entirely of coursed and dressed stone blocks, known as ASHLAR. This is exceptional, however, and most church stonework throughout the Middle Ages is less regular and smooth, especially the rough walling known as RUBBLE. Inside and out, walling of this kind was not usually meant to be seen, but was originally covered with a coat of plaster or RENDERING. Later restorers (*see* p. 149) have often stripped these surfaces back to the stonework, a historically questionable policy that nonetheless may pay dividends because of the blocked openings and other hidden features that are sometimes exposed.

Although sculptural remains such as stone crosses and grave-covers are quite common in many regions, early Anglo-Saxon churches are scarce. This is partly because of the destruction that accompanied the Danish invasions of the C9 and C10. With the return of more settled times, church building resumed across England. Most of the surviving Anglo-Saxon fabric dates from these later centuries. It is often fragmentary or disguised, representing churches that have been modified, enlarged, or otherwise partly rebuilt.

One of the most easily recognizable ANGLO-SAXON MOTIFS is a way of treating the angles of the building, known LONG-AND-SHORT WORK. The individual stones (known as QUOINS) alternate between vertical and horizontal placing, so that they stand out from the coursing of the rest of the walls, especially when this was rendered over. Ordinary walling is sometimes laid in alternating diagonal courses, known as HERRINGBONE pattern. Windows are small, and often have their arches formed from a single stone. The window surrounds are SPLAYED externally and internally; an external splay is especially likely to indicate an Anglo-Saxon date. Other windows and openings may have triangular heads formed of flat

stones or reused bricks. Where a church has a tower, its windows are often paired, with a shaped stone BALUSTER as the central support.

A few late Anglo-Saxon churches can show a more consistent architectural treatment. The little ashlar-faced C11 church at Bradford-on-Avon (Wilts.) has BLIND ARCADING – architecture in relief – around its upper walls. At Barton-upon-Humber (Lincs.) the nave-cum-tower has tiers of superimposed blind arcading, the uprights of the upper tier rising without structural logic from the crowns of the lower arches. Extremes of diagonal pattern-making appear at Earls Barton (Northants), a comparable instance of illogical applied architecture. A simpler form is seen at Barnack church tower in Peterborough (Hunts.), where thin vertical strips run all the way up. These thin members are known as LESENES, or alternatively as PILASTERS, a more common term which extends to columns of any style represented in flat relief.

6, 7. St Lawrence, Bradford-on-Avon, Wiltshire (left) and the tower of All Saints, Earls Barton, Northants, show contrasting late Anglo-Saxon styles of architecture in relief. Earls Barton also displays the long-and-short work on the tower angles, and multiple turned balusters in the belfry

8. The Anglo-Saxon crypt at St Wystan, Repton, Derbyshire. Probably of C8 or C9 origin, this well-preserved chancel crypt may have originated as part of a free-standing chapel

Most Anglo-Saxon CHURCH TOWERS are of the C10 or C11. The majority stand at the W end of the nave, as at Brixworth and Earls Barton. Variants include the church at Barton-upon-Humber, where the tower stood over the nave itself. A few churches have something like a crossing tower, that is to say a tower standing over the E end of the nave, to which the chancel and subsidiary N and S extensions or *porticus* are attached. Breamore in Hampshire and Repton in Derbyshire are examples of this Anglo-Saxon type. They differ from cross-plan churches built after the Norman Conquest of 1066 in that the lateral projections (also known as TRANSEPTS) and the chancel are all markedly narrower than the crossing tower itself, so that its corners project at the inner angles of the exterior. Repton also has an intact CRYPT, a feature of many of the more important Anglo-Saxon churches, including monastic churches. Such crypts are usually associated with the burial of saints or the display of relics.

The decorative treatment at Earls Barton has sometimes been interpreted as a stone imitation of WOODEN CONSTRUCTION, for it is known that many churches began as timber buildings. However, the only surviving example from the period has a very different look, having walls made of split logs placed upright between timber sills or beams. The church is at Greensted in Essex, and has been dated from tree-ring evidence to the late C11. Wooden construction has thus turned out to be another practice that continued in use for churches after the Norman Conquest, especially for smaller examples. Continuities of this kind explain the usage SAXO-NORMAN, and the period in architecture is sometimes referred to as the Saxo-Norman overlap.

One regional type well represented from this overlap is the ROUND TOWER. These are concentrated in East Anglia, where there are nearly two hundred, with an especially strong showing in Norfolk. Round towers are always placed at the W end of the nave. The form has sometimes been explained as a means of making best use of the local flints and other materials in areas without good building stone, because the absence of corners reduces the need for worked stone dressings. However, the existence of contemporary round towers on the Continent in areas of good building stone suggests that fashion had something to do with the phenomenon too. The type was still current into the C12, and a few examples date from as late as the C13.

2 NORMAN

The Conquest of 1066 transformed English architecture. All the cathedral churches and most of the great abbeys were rebuilt within a few generations, on a grander scale and in forms closer to the fully fledged ROMANESQUE manner of the Continent. Norman masons and churchmen drew especially on the ambitious and sophisticated architecture of Normandy itself, which remained in the hands of England's new rulers until the early C13. Parish churches were founded and rebuilt in large numbers too, in place of the old minster arrangement, and every English county has substantial survivals from this period – roughly, from just after 1066 to the late C12. The survival of so many well-documented great churches from this period onwards also makes it easier to track the spread of architectural ideas to parish level.

9. St Mary Magdalene, Cambridge. A well-preserved two-cell Norman church of c. 1150–70. Characteristic details include the doorway and window ornaments, decorated string courses, simple chamfered plinth, and angle rolls to the nave corners

▲ 10. All Saints, East Meon, Hampshire. A grand mid-C12 cruciform church with a crossing tower. The w doorway and tower retain their round-headed compound arches. The windows, s aisle and porch are mostly C13–C14 additions or insertions, but the timber broach spire may be as early as the mid-to late C12

The standard PLAN for most churches remained a simple two-cell arrangement of nave and chancel, though now with the thicker walling favoured by the Normans, while later Anglo-Saxon churches favoured square E ends. St Mary Magdalene, Cambridge, is a good example, in this case not a parish church originally but the chapel to a long-lost leper hospital. Chancels of Norman churches sometimes ended in a rounded apse, echoing the usual form of the E ends of greater churches of the period. Some small churches combined nave and chancel within a single rectangular enclosure, as may still be seen at Edstaston in Shropshire.

More ambitious parish churches may have a w tower, or sometimes a tower standing at the junction between tower and nave. The latter arrangement was more common in Norman times than it ever was under the Anglo-Saxons. In such cases the space under the tower may belong to the chancel or to the nave. In the former type, the E arch through the tower doubled as the chancel arch; in the latter, there may also be arches opening from the tower into transepts projecting to N and s, making a cruciform plan.

In place of the Anglo-Saxons' characteristic rows of *porticus*, the largest Norman parish churches have continuous AISLES to the nave. This is another form that can be traced back to the basilicas of the early Church, although it remained uncommon in English parish churches until the second half of the C12. The divisions between nave and aisles are made by ARCADES of free-standing piers or columns, with a half-column or RESPOND where they meet the end wall. A few ambitious C12 churches were built with both transepts and aisles, as at Hemel Hempstead (Herts.), or with aisles to the chancel, as at St Mary, Eastbourne (Sussex).

ARCHES of the period are round-headed, or occasionally have a depressed or elliptical profile; or they may be STILTED, i.e. raised on vertical pieces above the impost. These variants are more likely to appear in chancel arch rather than the arcades. Straight- or segment-headed door-way openings may also appear, set under a round-headed, solid arch (known as a RELIEVING ARCH).

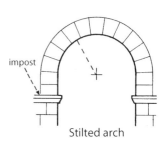

impost

Stilted arch

Wall surfaces are mostly plain, but there may be broad, shallow buttresses or pilasters, which share with the Anglo-Saxon version the alternative term LESENES. From the late C12, some larger towers

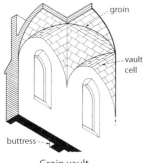

groin

vault cell

buttress

Groin vault

were built with shallow wall-thickenings to strengthen each corner, known as CLASPING BUTTRESSES.

Norman apses and towers, and sometimes chancels too, may have simple VAULTS of stone, either the plain forms known as BARREL (or TUNNEL) VAULTS and GROIN VAULTS (where two tunnel vaults intersect at right angles), or early RIB VAULTS (*see* p. 62). Where a chancel is vaulted only in part, as those with apses often are, the vault may help to define the area around the altar, known as the SANCTUARY.

A small but intriguing group of ROUND CHURCHES survives from this period, including two parochial buildings, in Cambridge and Northampton. Each consists of a round C12 nave attached to a rectangular (and rebuilt) chancel. The form was imitated from the churches of the Knights Templar, a crusading order who were the guardians of the circular-plan church of the Holy Sepulchre in Jerusalem. The order's London church has also survived, and now serves the legal enclave known as the Temple.

Few ROOFS of the period remain. What evidence we have suggests that they were often ceiled or boarded across, like those known to have been provided in greater churches. However, the roof at Kempley church in Gloucestershire – the oldest example yet identified, of *c.* 1120–50 – is unceiled, and consists of close-set trusses of a kind familiar from the C13 (*see* pp. 75–6).

Norman MASONRY becomes steadily more precise, including the thinness of its jointing. Architectural details too became more exact, and also sculpturally richer. The greatest show was usually reserved for the main doorway, which in most cases is placed on the S side, and for the CHANCEL ARCH, i.e. the opening between nave and chancel. Windows and bell-openings were also sometimes singled out for ornament. As with Anglo-Saxon churches, Norman WINDOWS tend to be both extremely small and widely spaced, whereas the openings in the upper stages of the tower are more likely to be grouped or paired.

11. St John, Yaverland, Isle of Wight. A mid-c12 chancel arch of compound type, with colonnettes intact

Doorways and chancel arches of the period (Anglo-Saxon ones too) are commonly of COMPOUND form: the form is doubled or multiplied as a sequence of concentric arches, and the uprights are multiplied to match. These are characteristically stepped inwards, and have separate COLONNETTES to support each subdivision of the arch, where it meets the IMPOSTS or blocks from which it springs.

The PIERS or columns of Norman arcades are usually plain and of circular section, but may be ornamented with devices such as FLUTING or spiral decoration. There is a good group of this type in north-east England, under the local influence of Durham Cathedral. Alternatively, the piers may be of thick square section, with or without decoration of the corners, or there may be alternating arrangements of piers and/or columns. ARCADING may also appear in relief on the exterior, as on the sophisticated c12 church

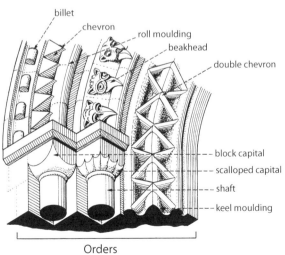

billet
chevron
roll moulding
beakhead
double chevron

block capital
scalloped capital
shaft
keel moulding

Orders

◀ 12. Part of the nave arcade of St Laurence, Pittington, Co. Durham. A late C12 example of the influence of a great church – in this case Durham Cathedral – on parish architecture

at Barfrestone in Kent. Sometimes the arches are INTERLACED, although the best examples of interlacing in parish churches are mostly found on fonts (*see* p. 26).

CAPITALS in early Norman churches are often simple shaped blocks, known as BLOCK or CUSHION CAPITALS. When this form has upright, widely spaced incisions, the capital is said to be SCALLOPED. Capitals may also feature small sculpted figures or scenes, sometimes known as HISTORIATED CAPITALS, or the little scroll-like forms called VOLUTES derived ultimately from classical designs. But the greatest displays of sculpture are usually to be found at the s doorway, in the TYMPANUM (the round-topped space over the doorway, enclosed by the arch). These include explicitly Christian scenes, such as the Lamb of God or Christ in Glory, as well as mysterious displays of monsters and serpents, thought to represent forces of evil which the Church keeps at bay.

◀ 13. St Peter and St Paul, Dinton, Buckingham-shire, engraved in 1847. A richly decorated compound-arched doorway of the mid C12, with a sculpted tympanum showing two beasts or monsters apparently eating from a Tree of Life

14. All Saints, Crondall, Hampshire. An ambitious aisled church of *c.* 1170–1200, with an interior juxtaposing late Norman and Transitional work. The aisles still display the characteristic Norman scalloped capitals and round arches, but the chancel and sanctuary arches and windows are pointed, with the Norman chevron motif as the chief ornament

The vocabulary of Norman ORNAMENT steadily expanded, especially in the C12. One of the easiest forms to recognize is the zigzag motif known as CHEVRON. This appeared in great churches from *c.* 1110 and soon spread to parish level. By the late C12 it had developed variants of powerful complexity, sometimes projecting diagonally, sometimes stepping inwards in right-angled sequence. A little later in origin is the distinctive English form known as BEAKHEAD, comprising animal heads or masks carved as if biting the individual stones or VOUSSOIRS of the arch. Sculpture and architecture are fused most powerfully in the wiry mid-C12 work of the so-called Herefordshire School, which combined influences and motifs from sources as diverse as Scandinavia, France and north Italy.

Plainer types of ornament include the simple rounded form known as a ROLL MOULDING. When used on a corner, as for example on a buttress or the outer angle of the church building, these mouldings are known as ANGLE ROLLS.

Smaller Norman motifs include the little discontinuous cylinders known as BILLET MOULDING, and NAILHEAD, which takes the form of a row of small pyramids. Besides ornamenting doorways and windows, these motifs may both appear in STRING COURSES – narrow horizontal bands of

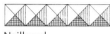

Nailhead

worked stone – around the church exterior. Some walls are finished with a CORBEL TABLE, made up of projecting blocks (corbels) that may take the form of sculpted heads. A corbel table allowed the roof to extend well beyond the plane of the wall, so that rainwater would be thrown clear.

Late C12 work that combines Norman and early Gothic forms (*see* p. 40) is known as TRANSITIONAL. A typical instance may display C12 motifs such as chevron around a pointed Gothic arch. Other tell-tale motifs from these decades are the WATERLEAF CAPITAL, with broad and simple leaf-like decoration (also used, inverted, on the corners of some square bases), the CROCKET CAPITAL, a version of an early French Gothic form, recognizable by its concave shape and short, stiff, prong-like projections, and the TRUMPET CAPITAL, with scalloped concave sides. Waterleaf may also appear on the square COLUMN BASES usually employed during the period, on the upper surfaces between the circular shaft and the right-angled corners. Some arches and openings of the late C12 already have curving projections known as CUSPS, a motif that becomes hugely important in the development of Gothic ornament.

Waterleaf

Crocket

impost block

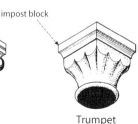

Trumpet

FONTS

A **font** is a vessel used for baptism, the ritual by which the Church receives a new member. Fonts are the earliest English church furnishing to survive in quantity, partly because they appear often to have been deliberately kept when the church was rebuilt around them. There are a few Anglo-Saxon survivals and many more Norman ones. The usual Norman form – also current into the C13 – is a simple tub shape, large enough to allow infant baptism by immersion. Other Norman fonts have square basins on round shafts. From the late C12 square or round bowls are sometimes set on multiple shafts, commonly one large central shaft surrounded by four smaller ones. At Bodmin in Cornwall this form is developed into an elegant, downward-curving bowl, with rich foliage carving.

Unusual materials include the black stone from present-day Belgium known as Tournai marble, and cast lead. Norman fonts in these materials include some richly sculpted examples, such as the lead font with the Signs of the Zodiac and the Labours of the Months at Brookland, Kent. More common as a form of ornament is simple arcading in relief. In the C13 this gave way to imitations of window tracery (see p. 56), and the usual form for the bowl became octagonal.

Later medieval fonts can usually be recognized from their chalice-like shape, with an octagonal stem of about the same height as the bowl. They may be decorated with small-scale architectural motifs, and sometimes with sculpted figures, such as the seated supporters (on the stem) and scenes representing the Seven Sacraments (on the bowl) that were popular in East Anglia. Some late medieval fonts have kept their tall, spired **covers** of wooden openwork. Exceptionally, medieval fonts may even sit within walk-in enclosures, like the C14 stone example at Luton, Bedfordshire.

Fonts survived the Reformation, as Protestantism retained the rite of baptism. Covers also remained in use; in some places, a replacement C17 cover will be found on a medieval font. However, during the C17 and C18 the basic form developed into slimmer outlines, sometimes approaching those used for secular furniture such as wine-coolers (Robert Adam's mahogany piece of the 1760s at Croome d'Abitot, Worcs., is an example).

15. The exceptionally ornate C12 font at St Petroc, Bodmin, Cornwall

Under the influence of the Gothic Revival, Victorian designers returned to medieval forms, sometimes deployed in inventive and original ways. Churches built since the Second World War are more likely to use simple, elemental forms such as rough-hewn stone blocks, although Evangelical congregations have come to prefer large sunken fonts or basins for adult baptism by total immersion.

▲   16. The lead font of c. 1200 at All Saints, Ashover, Derbyshire

▼   17. A late medieval font carved with the Seven Sacraments, from St Mary, Cratfield, Suffolk

3 ENLARGING CHURCHES

Medieval church buildings tended to grow as the centuries passed. There were many reasons for this. As the centre of parish life, the church was a source of pride and prestige, and it attracted both collective and individual patronage. Rising populations required more space. Competition with neighbouring parishes often also seems indicated, especially where grand towers and spires appear.

There were also specific reasons to expand. The development of ritual encouraged enlargement of the chancel, sometimes by eastward extension, sometimes by complete rebuilding. Many apses disappeared in the process, replaced by square E ends. Chancels of all periods often include a PRIEST'S DOOR, generally on the S side. Facilities for the priest might be provided by means of a VESTRY or SACRISTY. These were usually built as lean-to attachments with access from the chancel, especially on the N side. They can be distinguished from chapels by the small size of their doorways and windows.

Chancels may also be provided with a LOW-SIDE WINDOW: a tall window typically of the C13 or C14, which comes down unusually low. Where the window is divided horizontally by a TRANSOM, the lower part will often be found to have internal rebates for a lost shutter, which was probably used to ventilate the church after services. To provide better sight-lines for those in the nave or transepts, a plain SQUINT or viewing hole was sometimes cut through a wall or pier, aligned on the altar.

NAVES were also enlarged. An unaisled nave with an off-centre tower arch or chancel arch is likely to have been widened on one side. Westward extensions may reveal themselves by breaks in the stonework, or, where a church is aisled, by changes in the details or overall design of the arcade piers. Sometimes the builders left a slim section of plain wall before continuing with a new section of arcade. A cruder method was simply to punch one or more plain

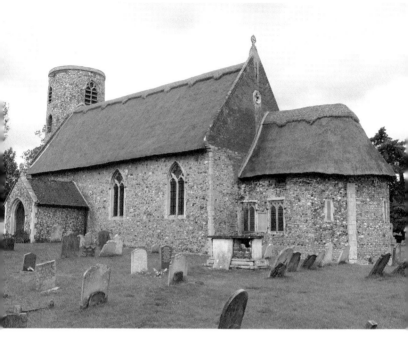

18. St Edmund, Fritton, Suffolk (now Norfolk). The lopsided plan is the result of widening the nave on one side only during C14 rebuilding. The apsed chancel and round tower are both C12, with some inserted C14 or C15 windows. About a hundred English churches are still thatched, most of them in Suffolk or Norfolk

arched openings through the side walls, without providing piers or responds.

An AISLE may be a single addition. Where aisles are present on both sides, they may be of different dates: it has been argued that the N aisle is more often the earlier, possibly because the s side of the churchyard was preferred for burials. Narrow aisles are a reliable sign of an early date; the C13 example at Limpsfield in Surrey is just eight feet wide. Existing aisles were often rebuilt wider, so that the outer walls are later in date than the arcades within. There may be evidence of this in the end walls of the aisle, in a break in the masonry or where the original window survives off-centre, especially at the w

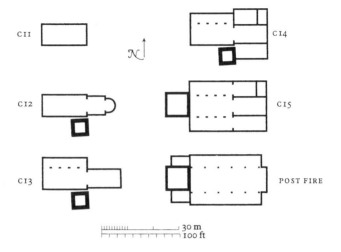

CII

CI2

CI3

CI4

CI5

POST FIRE

N

30 m
100 ft

▲   19. The development of St Bride's church, City of London, as revealed
by excavation. The placing of the big CI2 tower SE of the nave is
unusual. Sir Christopher Wren reused much of the late medieval
foundations when the church was rebuilt after the Great Fire of 1666

end. Conversely, arcades were frequently rebuilt leaving the existing aisle walls in place, such as when a new roof was provided over
the nave. Less drastically, existing arcades could be heightened by
inserting extra courses in the shafts, as at St Cuthbert's church in
Wells (Somerset). A less elegant economy was adopted by the late
medieval masons working at Skidbrooke church in Lincolnshire,
who chose to heighten its C13 arcade by resetting the stubby original
piers on bases almost as tall.

The majority of AISLE ROOFS slope upwards to the nave, on
the lean-to principle. Wider aisles are more likely to have double-
pitched roofs, i.e. with a gable at each end. The effect is magnified
in those large churches, especially in towns, which have double
aisles on one or both sides. In these cases the nave may have ended
up wider than it is long, usually a sign that sideways enlargements
have outpaced any increases in length from W to E. This may indicate where a street or public passage made an immovable barrier to

▲ 20. St John Baptist, Berkswell, Warwickshire, clearly displays its multiple phases externally. The chancel is well-preserved late C12 work, with an intact corbel table and the unique feature of an octagonal crypt below. The nave is of several phases including a s aisle of c. 1300, the tower is C15, the timbered s porch is C16

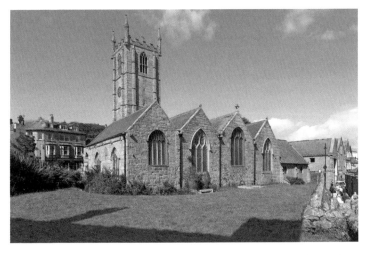

▲ 21 St Ia, St Ives, Cornwall. An aisled church of 1410–34 with an additional s aisle of c. 1500, indicated by the different window profile

growth in the expected direction. An urban church tower with open arches to N and S, like that of St Peter Mancroft in Norwich, usually shows where a right of way formerly ran through. For similar reasons, a town church may have its tower placed to one side, where there is no room for it to project centrally from the W front.

The doorway of an aisle is not always a safe guide to the date of the remainder, as it was quite common for doorways to be taken down and reused. Sometimes aisles swallowed up older transepts or side chapels, or merged with them. Aisles could also be extended alongside the tower, and sometimes alongside the chancel, although these eastward extensions generally functioned as separate chapels rather than as part of the shared space of the nave. Chapels of this kind may sometimes have a CRYPT, especially in a town church.

An internal arch across an aisle may mark the point at which a former transept or chapel has been incorporated. In other cases, arches may have been provided to strengthen the aisle, perhaps inserted later in response to settlement. A single-sided arch in this position, called a FLYING ARCH, works on the same principle as a flying buttress (*see* p. 40), steadying the inner wall against sideways movement.

PORCHES were common additions, especially from the C13. Thus a Norman doorway may now be framed by the outer doorway of a C13 porch, or a C13 doorway by a C14 porch. Some porches are of two dates, having been enlarged with an upper storey. Timber porches are locally common in some southern and western counties. These may retain some carved decoration, especially on the BARGEBOARD of the gable and in the traceried openings to the sides. The most common location for a porch is the second bay from the W, close to the usual position for the font. Where N and S porches or doorways are present, as was common from Norman times onwards, they are usually aligned with one another across the nave. BENCHES of stone are common presences along the porch walls inside, and there may be a STOUP to contain holy water by the inner door (or just within).

Many aisled churches have been heightened by means of a CLERESTORY above the arcades, allowing more light into the central vessel of the nave. The walls above the arcades may even contain blocked windows from an earlier and lower clerestorey, made

22. The timber w porch at St John the Baptist, Aconbury, Herefordshire, probably C15. The church is C13

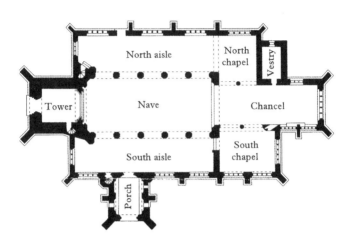

redundant by later heightening of the nave or aisles. Clerestoried churches are commonplace in all areas except the South West, especially Devon and Cornwall, where the preference was to keep the nave, aisles and chancel of near-equal height (thus often dispensing with a chancel arch altogether).

In most cases, where a clerestory was added a new roof was also needed (*see* pp. 74 and 96). Later medieval fashion preferred roofs to be of shallower pitch than those of the centuries before – a change sometimes captured on the W wall of the tower, where the outline or CREASE of the older, steeper roof may appear above the tower arch (or sometimes on the same wall above the existing roof line). These may also occur on re-roofed churches where a clerestory is absent. Evidence may also be found in the internal aisle walls in the form of corbels that once supported a roof of steeper pitch than the present one, or merely the scars where such corbels used to be. A more economical method was to take down and reuse the old corbels when the aisle walls were heightened, a practice that was sometimes also followed with external corbel courses.

The presence of a central tower is usually a sign that a parish church has early medieval origins, even if the TOWER itself may subsequently have been rebuilt. By the C14 the usual fashion was to place the tower at the W end instead, whether or not this was done

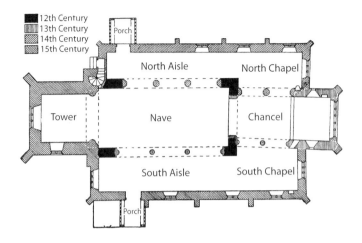

12th Century
13th Century
14th Century
15th Century

Porch

North Aisle   North Chapel

Tower   Nave   Chancel

South Aisle   South Chapel

Porch

▲ 23, 24. Contrasting histories could result in similar church plans. St Peter and St Paul, Northleach, Gloucestershire (left) was rebuilt to a consistent design from the late C14 to late C15. At the Berkshire church of St Andrew, East Hagbourne (right), parts remain of the C12 nave, widened with aisles and chancel chapels in several phases in the C13–C15, and with a W tower and chancel also of different dates. (Not to scale)

as part of a wider scheme of enlargement. A few churches with transepts and central towers were built here and there after the C13, as at Shottesbrooke in Berkshire, founded in 1337. Where the tower stands at the W end, it usually incorporates a centrally placed doorway in its W face – but not always, as some churches still depended exclusively on entry from the side. Sometimes a crossing tower was taken down in favour of a new tower at the W end, leaving thicker piers or sections of solid wall at the crossing as evidence of the original arrangement. Westward enlargement of a church which already had a W tower could be achieved by extending the aisles alongside it on one or both sides. A tower that is hemmed in like this often proves to be earlier than the aisles immediately alongside. Likewise, a tower standing at one angle of the nave or part-way alongside it may have been embraced by later aisles or chapels. In a few such cases the tower may originally have been free-standing; an arrangement which

▲ 25. St Andrew, Tarvin, Cheshire. A stalled scheme to rebuild the church in the early C16 has left the C14 chancel intact, with the wall of the big replacement N aisle cutting into it

survives best in the widely spaced counties of Norfolk, Herefordshire and Cornwall, which can muster sixteen examples between them.

Inside the church, a w tower commonly opens to the nave with a generously sized archway, known as a TOWER ARCH. These tended to increase in size as the centuries passed, and the w window in the tower, visible from inside the church through the arch, became correspondingly larger. Many church interiors thus have a balancing visual interest at both ends, the tower arch and window to the w and the chancel arch and altar window to the E. Similarly, the chancel arch was often rebuilt wider, so that it is quite common to find a late medieval arch in this position even when the wall between nave and chancel is structurally of the C12 or C13. Likewise the position of the chancel arch usually remained fixed even when the fabric of the church was completely rebuilt on either side, sometimes several times over.

Churches could also be reduced in size. Even in the Middle Ages, aisles or chapels were sometimes lopped off, especially in areas where plague, economic decline or agricultural change had shrunk the population. After the Reformation, side chapels in particular were vulnerable to removal. Their former presence may be revealed by a blocked-up arch at the E end of a transept, or on the flank of the chancel (sometimes signalled by a redundant piscina there; *see* p. 50). A lost transept or aisle may be indicated by the blocking-up of a transept arch or entire nave arcade. Sometimes the old windows were re-set in the infill walling, the material and workmanship of which may be the best guide to the date of the alteration. Chancels were sometimes removed too, or replaced with smaller ones, although in both cases Victorian initiatives have often supplied a full-scale replacement.

Enlargements were not the only way in which medieval churches could be enhanced. The single most common alteration was to replace a WINDOW (or windows) in an existing wall with a new one, designed according to the fashion of the day. Window types became larger as the years passed, so it was possible for a new opening to remove all traces of the window it replaced. In other cases the old windows may survive, blocked up but still visible from one or both sides, such as where a late medieval window has been knocked through the wall between two small Norman openings. Existing window openings could also be updated, so that the jambs or sill may turn out to be older than the tracery and the arch that accompany them. There is more on the different styles and types of window in the chronological chapters that follow.

DOORS

Medieval church **doors** survive in great numbers, especially in rural settings. Of special interest are those which are enhanced by decorative **ironwork**. The hinges in particular may be elaborated into C-shaped or serpentine patterns, the oldest of which belong to the C12. Lock-plates and handles may also be treated decoratively. After the mid C13, some smiths adopted the French technique of using dies to stamp the scroll-ends into uniform shapes, as at Turvey and Leighton Buzzard (Beds.). Sometimes the outer planks of a door simply have their nails arranged in ornamental patterns.

▼   26. The late C13 door and ironwork at All Saints, Turvey, Bedfordshire

Although old ironwork will sometimes be seen refixed on fresh timbers, a good many doors still have their original woodwork. Early medieval doors were built in two layers, the outer made up of vertical planks, the inner side of planks placed horizontally. Later medieval doors are more likely to depend for strength on braces spaced at intervals on the inner face, sometimes including diagonal as well as horizontal timbers.

The popularity of tendril and scroll forms for ironwork declined during the C14, as decorative interest shifted towards the planks of the door itself. These were carved with traceried patterns, imitating those used for windows, or sometimes with the late medieval motif known as **linenfold**, a Netherlandish invention that resembles sharp-folded cloth hangings. A simpler and more common treatment was to apply vertical timber mouldings to cover the joints between the planks of the outer face.

27. The N door at St Peter and St Paul, Clare, Suffolk, probably late C14

Where they survive, C17 and C18 doors can usually be recognized by the presence of large sunk **panels**, like those on doors of secular buildings of the period. Gothic decorative motifs in iron and wood begin to appear in the early C19, but a wholehearted revival of medieval construction methods and ironwork patterns had to wait for the Victorian decades. Sometimes a draught lobby will also be found just inside the door, especially in urban churches, where it may occupy the space under a W gallery.

Inner doors of **plate glass** have been introduced to a growing number of churches since the 1960s. They allow the interior to remain visible even when the church is locked, and may also be decorated with engraved imagery or lettering.

4 EARLY ENGLISH GOTHIC

The GOTHIC style developed in France in the late C12. In its fullest expression, it combined pointed arches, rib vaults and the diagonally slanting arches known as FLYING BUTTRESSES to create a new aesthetic of soaring volumes enclosed by structurally expressive, linear forms. England was quick to develop its own distinctive version of the style, commonly known as EARLY ENGLISH, and this remained current into the second half of the C13.

In parish churches, the most common motif of the period is the LANCET WINDOW, a single light with a TWO-CENTRED pointed head. Lancets may be paired or grouped together, especially for the E window, where three, five or even seven lights may be combined in a symmetrically stepped composition. The arches themselves are sharply pointed, or sometimes TREFOILED by means of a cusp on each side. Where the lancets are grouped close together, a RELIEV-ING ARCH sometimes extends over the heads of the group. Where a group of lancets is more widely spaced, the openings may be linked by a continuous string course that runs up and over the separate arch heads.

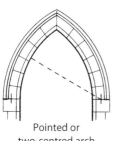

Pointed or
two-centred arch

lancet

Plate tracery

Some windows of the period are embellished with cylindrical SHAFTS of stone, especially where the lancets are set close together. These embellishments are more likely to be found inside the church than outside, both around the individual lights and sometimes on

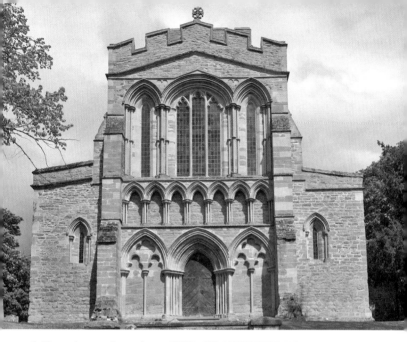

28. The early C13 w front of St Mary, Felmersham, Bedfordshire. Many characteristic Early English details appear, including blind plate tracery (below), lancet windows, grouped or clustered shafts, dogtooth ornament, and deeply moulded pointed arches. The crenellation and central window details are alterations

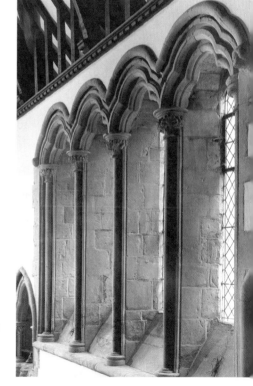

29. The chancel s windows at St Mary, Acton Burnell, Shropshire are lavishly treated inside, with trefoiled rere-arches and shafts of Purbeck stone. The date is c. 1270–80

▲ 30. St Andrew, Droitwich, Worcestershire, looking from under the N tower, through the chancel arch and into the nave. The C13 piers are of both octagonal and compound types, and the arches vary in richness from simple chamfering to full mouldings. Likewise the nave capitals have plain mouldings, those of the tower arches an ornamental combination of stiff-leaf and carved heads

the inner arch or RERE-ARCH as well. A similar arrangement of shafts was used to embellish doorways, carrying on from the general form used by the Normans. They may be interrupted by little stone discs known as SHAFT-RINGS, used originally to join separate stone pieces to make a single shaft, then adopted more generally as a decorative device. Especially in the South East and North East of the country these shafts may be of a contrastingly dark colour, notably Purbeck marble from Dorset (actually a fine-grained, near-black limestone) or the shell-studded Frosterley marble from County Durham.

Characteristic MOULDINGS of the period include the thin horizontal projections known as STRING COURSES. These are typically used to the link together the sills and heads of lancet windows, the upper string running unbroken up and over each window arch. But the richest mouldings in a C13 church are usually found in the compound arches over shafted doorways. Unlike the ornamented arches of Norman or Transitional date with their rhythm of repeated raised motifs, these complex and deeply undercut mouldings sweep continuously through the arch, so that a cross-section taken at any point will show an identical profile.

A later window type, dating from the second quarter of the C13, introduces simple piercings to the wall-space above and between the lancets. These piercings are known as PLATE TRACERY. Circular piercings are common, whether cusped or uncusped. A circle with cusps is described as FOILED, and the different types are identified by number: three cusps make a TREFOIL, four a QUATREFOIL, five a CINQUEFOIL, six a SEXFOIL, and so on. Foiled shapes, trefoils especially, may also appear without an enclosing circle, especially as a BLIND (unpierced) motif. The pointed-ended oval shape known as a VESICA may also appear in blind plate tracery.

Building skills continued to be passed down from the increasingly challenging projects undertaken for greater churches in the C13, with a corresponding increase in sharpness and precision in many areas. Walls became somewhat thinner, and more dependent on regularly spaced BUTTRESSES for strength. These are narrower than the Norman type, and project further from the wall surface, to which they are stepped inwards by means of SET-OFFS. When

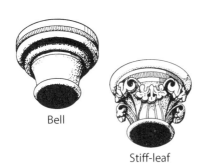

Bell

Stiff-leaf

placed at the corners of a church building, C13 buttresses are usually deployed in right-angled pairs known as ANGLE BUT-TRESSES. Where a church has an external PLINTH, i.e. a formalized thickening of the bottom courses of the wall, the upper edges (and sometimes the lower courses too) are more likely to be moulded than those of Norman churches. A simpler treatment is to finish the edge of the plinth with a plain diagonal CHAMFER. Whatever their date, most external plinths represent a thickening of the masonry in the foundations, and so they are often at their most elaborate around the tower, where the need is greatest.

The movement towards slimmer and less massive forms also left its mark inside. An influence from the lean, spare and spacious aisled halls of royal palaces and great houses has been detected in some of these churches, such as the mid-C13 nave at Stone in Kent. The PIERS of the arcades became slimmer, and their forms more diverse. One new form of the period has a circular central pier to which smaller shafts are attached; another is treated as a cluster of shafts of more equal size, typically giving a quatrefoil section. Sometimes the section of the individual shaft may be pointed or

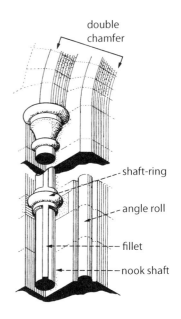

double chamfer

shaft-ring

angle roll

fillet

nook shaft

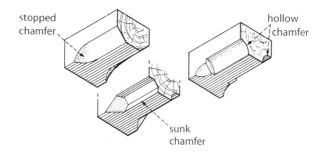

stopped chamfer

hollow chamfer

sunk chamfer

KEELED on its outer face, a motif first used in the late C12, or there may be a flat strip applied to the round surface, known as a FIL-LET (a slightly later form). Straightforward circular and octagonal pier sections continued in use too. CAPITALS are sometimes simple BELL SHAPES, or are ornamented with the unfurling plant forms known as STIFF-LEAF FOLIAGE, heavily stylized and more deeply cut than the crocket and volute types from which they evolved; as a rule, the leafier and lusher the foliage, the later the date. The square cap or ABACUS that which customarily topped off a Norman pier above the capital made way for a circular one, a form current into at least the mid C14. Most BASES of the period are circular too.

The arches of a C13 arcade are almost invariably pointed, and commonly chamfered at the edges. An arch of this type may be sin-gly or doubly stepped, in which case it is described as DOUBLE- or TRIPLE-CHAMFERED. From the later C13, the chamfering of some arches was finished above the capitals with little upright pieces known as BROACHES. The chamfering may also have a convex surface, known as a HOLLOW CHAMFER, and this too is slightly later in origin than the plain alternative form. Where the recess is straight-sided, it is known as a SUNK CHAMFER; this is less com-mon in arcade arches. A chamfer that slopes back to a right-angled edge is said to be STOPPED. All of these chamfered forms are also commonly found on woodwork, as illustrated above.

The richest type of arches may display the complex continu-ous mouldings already described in connection with doorways.

△ 31. A late C13 headstop from the nave arcade of St Catherine, Litling-
ton, Cambridgeshire

Sometimes the arcades have slim relieving arches, and these may
spring from HEADSTOPS, some of which take the form of ideal-

ized or (less often) grotesque sculpted
heads. A common ornamental device
that may appear almost anywhere is the
Dogtooth
row of little pointed square star-shapes
known as DOGTOOTH.

The C13 also brought a more ambitious approach to SPIRES.
These appear to have developed out of the pointed ('SADDLE-
BACK'), pyramidal, or HELM-type roofs used on Romanesque
church towers, of which England has far fewer than many
Continental countries. Spires may be of stone, or of timber faced
with lead or wooden shingles. As a rule, medieval stone spires
follow the belt of superior building stone that stretches from the
Bristol Channel to the Humber, with especially good showings in
Oxfordshire, Northamptonshire and Lincolnshire. Timber spires
were formerly more common than now, being more vulnerable than

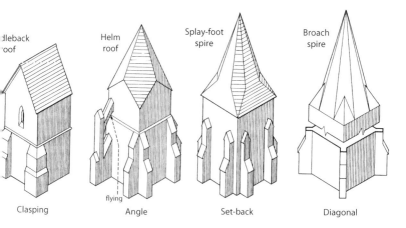

dleback
oof

Helm
roof

Splay-foot
spire

Broach
spire

Clasping

Angle

flying

Set-back

Diagonal

stone to damage and decay; they are also much less likely to make a show of decorative details.

The most noticeable of these details are the gabled, window-like openings known as LUCARNES. In a stone spire these characteristically appear at more than one level, diminishing as they rise, and sometimes alternating between the diagonal and the cardinal faces. Large, low-set lucarnes may double as bell-openings, as at Ringstead (Northants), although in most cases their chief practical use must have been for ventilation. Here and there, spires also appear with cusped circular piercings instead of full lucarnes; the largest concentration of these is in Leicestershire.

The characteristic English spire shape is octagonal in section. It may be carried down directly on to the edges of the tower, or it may be set back behind a parapet. The commonest treatment used in the C13 was the BROACH SPIRE, in which the parapet is omitted. Spires of this type intersect with shallower-pitched sections at the base, known as broaches. These are effectively like sections of a pyramid intersecting with the octagon, each broach representing one angle of the pyramid, and tapering to a point against the spire's diagonal faces. A variant especially popular in the East Midlands is the SPLAY-FOOTED spire. Here the cardinal faces of the spire are splayed outwards at the base so that they meet at each corner of the tower. The diagonal faces are terminated with solid pieces in the

▲ 32. All Saints, Buckworth, Huntingdonshire (now Cambridgeshire) has a late C13 broach spire with three diminishing tiers of lucarnes

33. A C13 variant on the simple broach spire at St Mary, Witney, Oxfordshire, where the corners of the tower are filled with big stone pinnacles in place of broaches

form of inverted triangles, and these adopt a shallower slope, so that each piece diminishes to its apex at the corner of the tower.

A rarer type combines an octagonal spire with an octagonal top stage of the tower. In such cases the transition to the octagonal form is often managed by means of PINNACLES at the angles of the square stage of the tower, as at Barnack in Peterborough (Hunts.). There are also a few C13 spires in which big pinnacles stand on all four tower corners right next to the spire, as at Witney (Oxon). Yet another possibility was to build the tower with octagonal buttresses at each corner, which could likewise be used as the bases of pinnacles placed alongside the spire. There is a fine C13 example at Long Sutton in Lincolnshire, in which both pinnacles and spire are of lead-faced timber.

Even where a spire is recessed well behind the tower parapet, broaches are usually present, in order to marry the two parts structurally. This applies especially to stone-built spires. Sometimes these discreet broaches may be glimpsed in more distant views.

A few churches have octagonal or polygonal tops without an accompanying spire. Some of these, especially those of late medieval date, were never meant to have spires, but to finish in a light and airy stage of pierced stone. A windowed or openwork top stage of this kind is called a LANTERN. Two of the best-known examples are the 'Boston stump' in Lincolnshire and All Saints Pavement church in York.

Elsewhere in the counties bordering Scotland, churches and church towers were built with DEFENCE in mind. An extreme example is the church at Newton Arlosh in Cumbria (formerly Cumberland), built in the early C14 when Anglo-Scottish warfare was endemic. Its broad, thick-walled and slit-windowed tower has a vaulted ground stage, and can be entered via the nave. The arrangement is similar to the contemporary tower houses of the region, with a nave in place of a domestic hall.

Churches without towers made do with a simple pierced BELL-COTE of wood or stone, customarily placed on top of the w gable. These remained current to the end of the Middle Ages and beyond. A bellcote over the chancel arch was usually intended for the special purpose of ringing a bell during the consecration of the Mass, and is known as a SANCTUS (holy) BELLCOTE.

Two smaller features that become increasingly common from the C13 onwards, and which belong physically as much to the architecture of the church as to its furnishings, are piscinas and sedilia. A PISCINA is a stone recess used for washing the vessels of the Mass, for which a shallow basin and drain were provided in the sill. It has an arched head, and may include a stone shelf called a CREDENCE SHELF. Sometimes the piscina comprises two arched openings side by side. A PILLAR PISCINA is an early form, most common in the C12, in which the basin is placed on a shaft rather than cut into the wall.

SEDILIA (singular: sedile) are seats used by the clergy. These are almost always set into the s wall of the chancel in vertically divided groups of up to four, and usually are usually stepped upwards towards the altar end. They may be grouped with the piscina, and both may be richly ornamented with shafting, carving, etc. Piscinas may also be found in aisles and chapels, mid-way along a lengthened

▲ 34. The sedilia and piscina (left) of c. 1320 at St Catherine, Faversham, Kent are combined in a single design, with some of the rich and playful carved ornament associated with the Decorated style

chancel, at the E end of the nave, and anywhere else in which an additional altar originally stood.

Any small, unornamented rectangular recess in the chancel wall is likely to have begun as an AUMBRY, a lockable cupboard where the sacred vessels were kept. Especially in some eastern counties, there may also be an EASTER SEPULCHRE in the chancel N wall. The Easter sepulchre was a medieval representation of Christ's tomb, used as part of the Easter rituals. Its usual form resembles a tomb recess (*see* p. 69) built into the chancel wall to display the effigy, and in certain cases these recesses were enhanced with architectural adornments and sculpted figures. The well-known mid-C14 example at Hawton, Nottinghamshire, even has sleeping soldiers carved in niches in its base. Cowthorpe church in Yorkshire (West Riding) has an exceptional canopied mid-C15 example of timber, in which the lower part doubles as the parish chest.

The open appearance of many medieval churches today is deceptive, for they were originally subdivided by **screens**. The indispensable location was across the western end of the chancel, making a firm physical division between the priest's domain and that of the laity in the nave. This was known as a **rood screen**, after the carved or painted Crucifixion group that was customarily displayed above it until the Reformation ('rood' is the Anglo-Saxon word for cross).

Timber was the usual material for screens in parish churches, although a few stone ones survive, such as the C14 example at Ilkeston in Derbyshire. Whatever the material, the arches or square-headed bays on either side of the screen's central doorway were provided with openwork tracery. The lower zone of the screen was commonly filled with solid panelling with carved tracery, often with painted figures of saints. Where the **mullions** or upright members in the openings of a timber screen are not moulded or straight-edged but turned, i.e. of circular section, the work can be dated before the C15.

Screens exhibit strong regional differences. The West Country favoured screens running straight across the church from wall to wall, thus creating chapels in the E extensions of the aisles. In northern England, the familiar Perpendicular forms may be replaced with the more fluid patterns of the Flamboyant style, a sign of Continental influence (*see* p. 83).

Here and there, the **rood loft** may survive too. This is a narrow upper walkway or gallery, formerly used to gain access to the rood figures and also as a vantage point for singing, and almost everywhere built integrally with the screen itself. As the loft was deeper than the screen, it was usually made to project towards the nave by means of panelled **coving** or timber vaulting, both of which may be richly carved. The loft part too may be handsomely embellished, sometimes by means of the pierced openwork cresting known as **brattishing**.

Even when both rood screen and loft have gone completely, their former presence may be betrayed by the **rood stair** that once provided access to the upper level. As the fully developed rood loft was a relatively late feature, these stairs may appear as insertions or additions in older fabric, typically as a square or polygonal projection near the external junction of nave and chancel. In areas such as East Anglia, where brick came into favour in the C15, the rood stair may be of that material even when the rest of the walls are stone-built. Where the screen ran right across the church, as in many West

▲ 35. The stone screen at Ilkeston, Derbyshire, a rare survival from the early C14. The slim mullions and bar tracery are similar to the forms of some contemporary woodwork and metalwork

Country churches, the rood stair may be found built into the thickness of an aisle wall. Either or both of the doors to the stair, lower and upper, may be visible in the nave inside wall (an internal doorway that opens mysteriously high up in the wall here is almost always a relic of one). Sometimes the staircase is visible too, often as the result of reopening by a Victorian restorer.

Parclose screens were used to define separate chapels within the church. They typically make right-angled enclosures at the E end of an aisle, or divide a transept from the main space. Specially rich C15 parclose chapels include those at Dennington (Suffolk) and Cirencester (Gloucs.), both with screens made of wood, as was customary. These side chapels might be dedicated to individuals or families who had endowed a **chantry** by which Masses were to

53

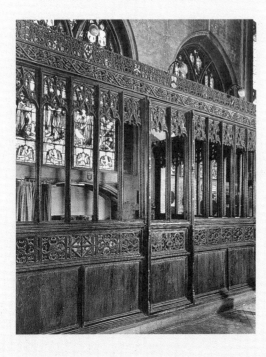

36. A parclose screen, from a side chapel at St John the Baptist, Cirencester, Gloucestershire. The date is c. 1460

37. A typical late medieval West Country screen, from St John, Carhampton, Somerset. The colouring dates from 1862, but is based on original traces

be said for the benefit of their souls, or belong to one of the many guilds or confraternities of lay people, who likewise arranged for services or Masses on their own behalf. **Stone-built chantry chapels** are much less common in the parishes than in cathedrals and other great churches, but exceptions exist, including a balancing early C16 pair by the altar of Newark church, Nottinghamshire.

Generally, screens from before the C15 are uncommon, and those from before the C14 exceptionally so. The largest concentration of screens of every medieval period is in East Anglia. A few tradition-conscious parishes installed them in the C17 and C18, including even a couple in the City of London from the rebuilding after the Great Fire of 1666.

However, the vast majority of **post-medieval screens** owe their origin to the Victorian and post-Victorian enthusiasm for the Middle Ages. Many of these follow English timber prototypes, but in some cases **wrought iron** was used to brilliant effect, breaking away from medieval precedent to achieve something genuinely original. Another crucial development, deriving from

the Ritualist movement of later Victorian times, was the revived practice of having more than one altar in a church. The multitudes of Lady Chapels, saints' chapels and war memorial chapels that this change made possible are often provided with their own screens, as well as other furnishings.

5 THE DECORATED STYLE

The DECORATED STYLE is the term commonly used to cover the version of Gothic that prevailed from the mid to late C13 to the mid C14. Its most recognizable motifs can be found in WINDOW TRACERY. This falls into two distinct phases, both of which derive from the development of BAR TRACERY from the plate tracery of the first half of the C13. By reducing the stonework between the lower lights to narrow mullions, and enlarging the upper openings so that the flat areas of infill gave way to a series of thin linear mouldings, a wealth of new types of window could be generated.

The earlier category is GEOMETRICAL TRACERY. This began with groupings of circular openings, often with foils or cusps. One

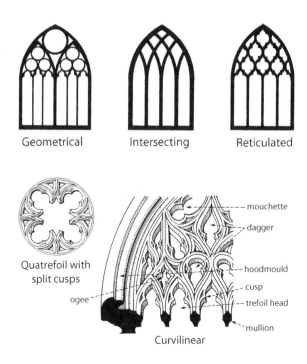

Geometrical   Intersecting   Reticulated

Quatrefoil with split cusps

ogee

mouchette

dagger

hoodmould

cusp

trefoil head

mullion

Curvilinear

38. A late Geometrical window from All Saints, North Moreton, Oxfordshire (formerly Berkshire), c. 1300–10, with original stained glass

common form used from *c.* 1250 has three lower lights: two circles on top, and a single circle in the apex of the arch. Windows with more than three lights permitted further variations, such as the combination of contrastingly large and small circular openings. In the later decades of the c13 the convention that circles should govern the tracery design was relaxed in favour of a wider variety of shapes, such as curved-sided triangles and trefoils, and quatrefoils without circular enclosures.

From around 1290, and especially after 1300, these regular forms relaxed into something more fluid and linear, hence the names FLOWING or CURVILINEAR TRACERY. One crucial innovation

▼ 39. St Mary, Cottingham, East Yorkshire (formerly East Riding). A cruciform church with an aisled c14 nave and c15 tower. The nave windows have Decorated tracery of curvilinear or flowing type, the tower openings show the straight-sided forms of the Perpendicular style

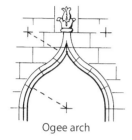

Ogee arch

was the pointed, reverse-curved form known as an OGEE. Ogee openings were too weak structurally to be used for major load-bearing openings, but the form was taken up with relish by makers and designers in every medium, from illuminated manuscripts to metalwork. Applied to tracery, it made possible a huge repertoire of curving, leaf-like shapes.

One memorable variant, especially popular around 1330, is the net-like form known as RETICULATED TRACERY. This has openings of equal size, which are frequently cut across by the main arch rather than fitting into it. Ogee forms also encouraged a more free treatment of the smaller apertures between the main tracery openings, which often adopted the tear-like forms known as MOUCHETTES or the pointed shapes known as DAGGERS. These playful and intricate effects were enhanced by elaborated cusping, including SUB- or DOUBLE CUSPING, by which smaller cusps are applied to the sides of large ones. SPLIT CUSPS have their points interrupted by V-shaped gaps, a variant especially common in Kent (hence the alternative name, KENTISH TRACERY).

One simpler form that can be found almost everywhere from the last years of the C13 onwards is INTERSECTING TRACERY, in which the lines of each pointed arch are continued into the window head, following the sweep of the outer arch. The same principle applied to a two-light window generates the simple form known as Y-TRACERY. Both kinds may be cusped or uncusped.

All these descriptions relate to windows of the most common type, namely of upright form and with a pointed arch. Other WINDOW SHAPES that became established in the C14, especially for aisles and the side walls of naves and chancels, include straight-headed oblong openings and those with shallow segmental arches (a much rarer form). For

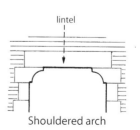

Shouldered arch

▲ 40. The exceptionally rich s aisle chapel at St Luke, Gaddesby, Leicestershire. Among many rich Decorated motifs of c. 1325–50 here are the ornamented battlements and flowing frieze, buttresses carried up as crocketed pinnacles, and multiple niches with ogee arches and miniature gables

further variety, Decorated windows in gables and other secondary wall surfaces were sometimes treated as segment-sided triangles, or given the circular or vesica shapes inherited from the Norman and Early English periods. Another late C13 addition to the repertoire of openings is the SHOULDERED-ARCHED DOORWAY, sometimes called a Caernarvon arch from its early use at Edward I's castle of that name.

The same impulse towards variety and lively outline can be traced in other parts of the church, especially in buildings of the more ambitious type, in which the exterior is treated as a single architectural composition. As well as the established form that dies into the upper part of the wall, buttresses were now more likely to be finished with a little gable (known as a GABLET), or to be carried up above the parapet in the form of PINNACLES. The tops of Decorated pinnacles may be pointed or wedge-shaped, and usually display the sprig-like foliage form known as crockets by way of decoration. Parapets – themselves increasingly common from this period onwards – may terminate in battlements, also known as CRENELLATIONS. These were taken over from defensive architecture, probably via their imitation on small-scale structures such as shrines and canopies, and may originally have been intended to evoke the walls of the Heavenly City.

With or without crenellations, the lower part of the parapet may be decorated with a carved FRIEZE. Popular motifs for C14 friezes include the running tendril pattern known as VINE SCROLL and the little globular bud-like shapes named BALLFLOWER. The latter is not confined to friezes, but may appear almost anywhere, including window mouldings and even the members of bar tracery. It is one of those motifs that vary in frequency from region to region, being especially popular in the West Midlands and West Country. Also common

Ballflower

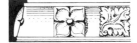

Fleuron

are the small, stylized four-leafed flowers known as FLEURONS, which may be spaced at intervals in a frieze, or used in continuous bands. The fleuron motif had a long life, with variations in use until the end of Gothic. By contrast, dogtooth and nailhead were no longer in general use by *c.* 1300. PERFORATED PARAPETS began in the C14, with motifs such as cusped triangles, and became still more elaborate in some regions in the C15 and early C16.

NICHES are another feature that proliferated in the period, especially in the C14. They may appear on the outer faces of buttresses, on

41. The tower vault of 1442–6 at All Saints, Lydd, Kent, showing the use of tierceron and lierne ribs

the fronts of porches, on either side of w doorways, or in balancing pairs on the inner E walls of chancels and aisles, to enhance the setting of an altar. In most cases they were meant to hold sculpted figures, some of which survive. Niches were also a perfect opportunity to indulge in the period's fondness for architecture in miniature. Many are provided with their own little pinnacles, and have elaborate ogee arches, or simple pointed arches under a crocketed ogee HOODMOULD (a projecting moulding to throw off rain). Sometimes the ogee form is developed into the three-dimensional shape known as a NODDING OGEE, in which the arch curves outwards and forwards to make a kind of enhanced canopy.

A miniature VAULT is another common embellishment of these niches. Vaults of greater or lesser scale allowed parish churches to display something of the same delight in pattern-making which

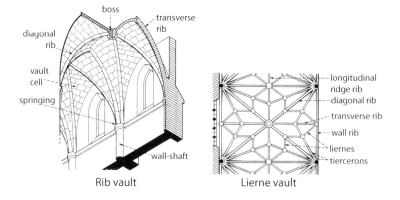

Rib vault   Lierne vault

characterizes full-scale structural vaults from the period. As developed under the Anglo-Normans, rib vaulting began with a simple fourfold pattern for each bay: diagonal ribs following the lines of the groining, bounded on each side by a TRANSVERSE RIB or CROSS RIB extending perpendicular to the walls. The crucial innovations were twofold. First was the introduction very late in the C12 of the TIERCERON, a secondary diagonal rib extending between the SPRINGING or starting point of the vault and its ridge or crown. The ridge was also given its own RIDGE RIB, and extra transverse ribs were added, following the summit of each vaulting bay from wall to wall. Secondly, these changes were followed in the late C13 by the LIERNE, a shorter type of rib that can connect the main and secondary ribs at any point, thus liberating the mason to create multiple variants of star- and cross-shaped patterns. Later Gothic vaults are also flatter in section than those of the first age of Gothic, and the ribs supporting them have a sharper profile.

Whatever the type, the intersections of ribs in a vault are commonly marked and reinforced by stone BOSSES. These are very often embellished with carving, including heads and figure groups.

Very few parish churches have vaults over their main spaces, but vaults in porches and towers are quite common in some regions. A vaulted porch is usually a sign that an upper storey, known as a PARVISE, is present. This might be used as a strong room, school, or living accommodation for the priest or church official; the

presence of a fireplace is a pointer to residential use. Vaults in towers usually serve to support the floor of a BELFRY or the ringing chamber below it, in which case there may be a large circular hole or holes in the vault to allow the bells to be hauled up, or the ropes to hang down. (The English custom of synchronized change-ringing by teams of bell-ringers standing within the belfry is post-medieval.)

Fine carving is also to be seen on CAPITALS of the period, which include some of the most rewarding in English medieval architecture. The varied formalized stiff-leaf types popular in the early C13 made way after c. 1260 for more naturalistic forms, sometimes immediately recognizable as a stone portrait of a native plant such as hawthorn or ivy. In the C14 the fashion shifted back to stylized foliage, especially an intricate but less deeply carved form which may resemble seaweed or some other knobbly undulating growth. Sometimes the carving appears to run in a continuous band around the projections and recesses of the capital, the form of which develops out of the shape of its supporting pier. A few churches have capitals incorporating sculpted heads or half-figures, instances of the animated playfulness of so much English art in this period.

PIERS show some strong continuities with earlier Gothic forms: types such as the quatrefoil section and plain octagon continued in use into the C14, although circular piers are dropped. In general, however, the projections and mouldings become shallower, giving the effect of a merging together of the separate shafts. In their simplest form, chamfered arches of the period may die into octagonal piers without any capital between, as at the C14 naves of St Mary,

▲ 43. St Mary, Snettisham, Norfolk. A C14 church of cruciform plan, with spectacular flowing tracery and a spire linked by flying buttresses to the corner pinnacles of the tower

Gateshead, and St Nicholas, Newcastle upon Tyne (now Newcastle Cathedral). In general, MOULDINGS of the period show a reduction in depth and number of hollows projections from the extremes of the C13, accompanied by a broadening of profile. Such forms as the WAVE and DOUBLE-WAVE moulding become common, as well as the shallow convex form known as a CASEMENT MOULD-ING, first used around the 1320s.

SPIRES remained in favour throughout the mid to late C13 and C14, a period which produced most of the finest English examples. As with church exteriors, the simpler outlines and types inherited from the early C13 were transformed and diversified with lively, broken outlines and small-scale stone ornament, especially crocket and ballflower. In more elaborate examples, broaches at the lower corners made way for complex arrangements of pinnacles, often set diagonally. These may also be paired one above the other, with little

▲ 44. St Mary, Upleadon, Gloucestershire. The timber-framed w tower of
c. 1500 is attached to a Norman nave. The chancel and s porch are Victorian

flying buttresses between each pair, or there may be flying buttresses
to link the corner pinnacles to the spire. Several of these forms may
be used in combination, as at the church of St Mary the Virgin in
Oxford.

In the absence of a full spire, there may be a small SPIRELET,
sufficient to carry a weathervane or a flagpole. Spirelets are usually of

timber, and lead-clad. Hertfordshire and the counties round about are a stronghold of this form, hence the term 'Hertfordshire spike'. They are difficult to date, but most are later than the C14.

TOWERS are incidentally one of the easiest parts of a church in which different phases can be detected, given that the lower parts must always be earlier than what may have been added on top. It is quite common to find that the lowest stage or stages are Norman or Early English and the belfry stage and spire (where present) Decorated, or later still. Or it may be that battlements have been added to an older tower, as this embellishment was not used on churches before the C13. Buttresses are another common addition, especially where a tower has been heightened. They may be found to cut across older features such as plinths, or betray their age by the lack of shared bonding and coursing with the stonework of the tower proper.

Phased construction of this kind does not necessarily represent heightening, as towers were sometimes built with a timbered upper stage that was subsequently replaced in stone. The combination survives at Holmer in Herefordshire, where the tower stands detached to the s of the nave. In addition, a few churches still have towers that are entirely TIMBER-FRAMED, such as Upleadon in Gloucestershire. This is in other respects a w tower of the usual type, but Herefordshire, Kent and Essex can show a few bell-towers wholly or partly of timber which memorably adopt stepped, pagoda-like forms. Their dates range from the late C12 to *c.* 1500; some are of the wholly free-standing type. High Halden in Kent has a stepped and shingled timber tower, complete with spire, that is attached to the nave in the usual way; it dates from the late C14. Other village churches in Kent, Surrey and Essex have timber-framed bell-turrets or small towers supported on massively framed timber posts, placed within the masonry walls of the nave.

The handful of wholly TIMBER-FRAMED CHURCHES of the C14 and C15 also deserve mention here. They are concentrated in the Welsh borders, with the majority in Cheshire. Where the nave is aisled, as at Marton and Lower Peover, the arcades are inevitably of timber too, like those of a great hall or barn.

Many church enlargements or rebuildings were paid for by individual patrons. In return, these patrons and their families could expect to be buried in an honoured place within. Especially from the C13 onwards, such gifts were likely to be commemorated by means of a monument (which may also double as a true tomb, or stand above a tomb). In addition, many ordinary burials of priests, knights, and sundry lay people were commemorated by a monument or permanent marker of one sort or another. Some of these were placed outside the church, and may remain there; others have since been brought inside for protection, but may show weathering that betrays their centuries spent outdoors.

Sculpted monuments in parish churches developed from so-called **coffin lids**. These can be traced back to the grave markers of Anglo-Saxon times, but became especially common in the C13. Some are simple flat stones, others are raised or ridged along the centre line. The usual decoration is some form of cross, sometimes with elaborate foliation to the ends. There may also be an emblem of the deceased, such as a sword for a knight or a chalice for a priest.

◀ 45. A collection of coffin lids or cross-slabs of the simplest medieval type, from All Saints, Ryal, Northumberland

▶ 46. A mid-C14 monument to an unknown lady from St Mary, Silchester, Hampshire. The angel supporters and ogee-arched tomb recess are typical of the period

Effigies also began to appear in numbers in the C13. These are carved in shallow relief, or sometimes simply represented as incised outlines. By the C14 the fashion was to show figures sculpted in the round instead. Among the most memorable are those of knights with their legs crossed, about to draw their swords. (The tradition that crossed legs represent a crusader is spurious, but probably immortal.) By the late C14, however, the usual posture is symmetrical and static, with hands clasped in prayer. Most effigies are of stone, but a few oak examples survive, including a cluster in Essex.

Early effigies were often placed in a **tomb recess**, formed by a low, broad arch within the church wall. Tomb recesses may be internal or external. They are almost always placed towards the E end of the church, usually in the chancel or transepts. Some belong to the original architecture, and may indicate that the deceased was its patron. But tomb recesses were easily inserted in existing walls too, which explains how sequences in slightly differing styles may sometimes be found in a line along a single chancel wall. One variant takes the form of an open archway connecting the chancel with a chancel chapel alongside, arranged so that the tomb fills the lower part of the opening.

▲ 47. The double monument to Thomas Vaughan (d. 1469) and wife at
St Mary, Kington, Herefordshire. A refined and ambitious example of a table
tomb, carved from costly alabaster

Later **tomb-chests** developed increasing complexity and richness, as the
coffin-shaped plinths used for early effigies gave way to taller, rectangular
bases. These could be decorated with miniature architecture, especially
niches or repeated quatrefoils; the latter often enclose miniature shields
on which heraldry could be represented. The niches commonly have or had
their own population of little sculpted figures: either 'weepers' (mourners,
represented as living people), or angels, sometimes holding shields.

Rectangular bases also allowed secular monuments to display two
effigies, husband and wife, side by side. A male effigy with two accompanying
females usually represents a second marriage after the first wife's death.

Church monuments soon acquired **canopies** (as distinct from the relatively modest arches of the tomb recess). Spiky, gabled silhouettes were introduced in the C13, and are best seen now in cathedrals and other great churches. In the C14 and C15 flat-topped forms were commonly favoured instead, especially those with solid sides and a broad arch towards the front. One macabre variant occasionally adopted for high-status tombs in the C15 has a double-decked arrangement with a **gisant** or sculpted corpse at the lower level, as at Fyfield in Berkshire (now Oxon). Less ambitious tombs of the canopied, flat-topped type were in such demand by the end of the period that some London masons appear to have kept ready-made stocks of them. Many tombs across southern England are made wholly or partly of Purbeck marble, including those from London workshops.

Brasses offered an alternative to carved effigies. Sometimes they were displayed on tomb-chests, or on the back wall under the arch. This allowed the top of the tomb to be used as an altar for celebrating Masses on behalf of the deceased. More commonly, brasses were set directly into a Purbeck marble slab in the floor (the stone setting of a brass is called a **matrix**). These were affordable across a broader social range than sculpted monuments, especially as brassmakers offered a wide choice of sizes, from over-life-size

▼ 48. Monument to Sir John Golafre (d. 1442) at St Nicholas, Fyfield, Oxfordshire (formerly Berkshire)

to miniature figures less than a foot long. It is very common to find a matrix that has lost most or all of its brasses, but even so, England preserves more church brasses than any other country.

Early brasses may show crosses or individual letters, but **figured brasses** begin to proliferate from the early C14. The earliest known double brass of a husband and wife is of the 1340s (Westley Waterless, Cambs.). Canopies or frames of architectural character appear at the same period, treated as separate insets to the matrix. The usual convention was to show the figures frontally, but from the C15 some are represented in three-quarters view or turned slightly sideways. Brasses were embellished with areas of colour, and a handful retain traces of the original paint or enamel.

Where a brass is treated as a single plate or plates combining both frame and effigy or pictorial scene, it may be an import from the Low Countries, where this type was more in favour. The all-in-one engraved plate was adopted by English makers in the C16 and C17, but these are usually small and artistically inferior to medieval Netherlandish work. Brasses made after the Reformation may also be **palimpsests**, i.e. engraved on the reverse side of older brasses that may have come from abolished churches or chapels.

Besides their artistic and historical interest, tomb effigies and brasses are a vital source for the history of costume, including armour and priestly vestments. In turn, monuments that lack inscriptions can be dated, and sometimes individually identified, by following clues in their sculptural style and details of dress. This scholarly approach may challenge traditional identifications, some of which depend on heraldic details identified over-precisely by long-dead antiquaries. Another trap for the unwary is the medieval custom of commissioning monuments during the subject's own lifetime, sometimes given away by a blank space left for the date of death.

49. An unusually complete double brass from St Milburga, Wixford, Warwickshire. The subjects are Thomas de Cruwe (d. 1411) and wife

6 CHURCH ROOFS TO c. 1400

ROOFS survive in some numbers from the C13 onwards. Almost all of them are of oak. The number that can be firmly dated has expanded hugely since the late 1970s thanks to the new technique of dendrochronology (tree-ring dating), which can sometimes identify the exact year in which timbers were cut and worked. Detailed studies have also shown that church roofs were renewed or drastically renovated more often than might be expected, as for instance when early structural failure required a roof to be taken down and remade with a proportion of new timbers. Dendrochronology has also demonstrated that older techniques continued here and there alongside newer ones for longer than had been assumed. On balance,

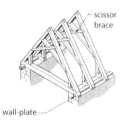

Scissor truss roof (single-framed)

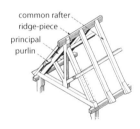

Kingpost roof (double-framed)

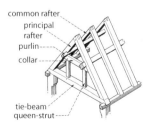

Queen-strut roof (double-framed)

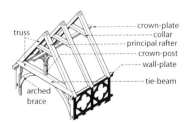

Crown-post roof (double-framed)

50. The interior of St Thomas, Winchelsea, Sussex, of c. 1285–1315. The single-framed roof over the central vessel is strengthened by arch-braced tie-beams over the arcade piers. The present church represents the chancel of a much larger building that was never completed

however, the technique has tended to confirm the sequence of development already deduced by scholars from visible evidence of structural form, jointing and ornament.

C13 roofs typically have close-set trusses made of paired rafters, sometimes braced with crossed-over timbers (a form known as a SCISSOR TRUSS, hence a SCISSOR-BRACED roof). At this period roofs were still constructed without a horizontal timber along the ridge. Trusses were sometimes boarded or ceiled below, placing the roof in the class known as a WAGON ROOF, from a resemblance to the inside of an old-fashioned road wagon.

Roofs of C14 churches show a movement away from this pattern of close-set multiple trusses. The crucial distinction to be made here is between single and double framing. A SINGLE-FRAMED ROOF consists of individual pairs of rafters, each with or without internal bracing, that are held in place by the horizontal timber or WALL-PLATE at the head of the wall. A DOUBLE-FRAMED ROOF – a much stronger form – has extra horizontal members or PURLINS that run perpendicular to the rafters and join them together. This in turn allows the rafters to be spaced more widely. In connection with this development, it becomes possible to make a distinction between PRINCIPAL RAFTERS, which are variously braced or tied together to provide the roof with the trusses necessary for stability, and the lesser or COMMON RAFTERS between, which are joined only to the purlins and (at the ridge) to each other.

One simple form of double-framed roof achieves stability by means of a straight TIE-BEAM joining each pair of principal rafters at the base, from the middle of which a KINGPOST rises vertically to the top of the truss. The type will be familiar, for it has become standard in ordinary houses. Or there may be two uprights placed symmetrically and off-centre on the tie-beam, known as QUEEN-POSTS or QUEEN-STRUTS. These rise to support the rafters at the point at which they are joined to the purlins, where the truss may be strengthened by an upper cross-tie known as a COLLAR.

A variant of the kingpost type, especially common in south-east England (and associated more with houses than with churches), is the CROWN-POST ROOF. In this case the post reaches up only as far as the collar. This upper joint is shared with a longitudinal member called a CROWN PLATE, which runs horizontally from collar to collar below the apex of the roof. Curved BRACES extend upwards from the sides of the crown-post in all four directions, to both crown plate and collar (or sometimes downwards to the tie-beam, i.e. in the lateral direction only). This helps to create a visually complex form, which may be further enhanced by chamfering or simple moulding.

▶   51. St Fimbarrus, Fowey, Cornwall. An early C14 church which shows the characteristic West Country combination of nave and chancel into a single elongated space. The central arched and ceiled roof here dates from the C15

▲ 52. The C14 arch-braced roof of the Holy Rood, Sparsholt, Oxfordshire (formerly Berkshire), depicted in 1849. The engraver has exaggerated the pitch of the roof, which is spanned by single timbers without a joint at the ridge

More common in churches in most areas is the ARCH-BRACED ROOF. This dispenses with the lower tie-beam in favour of pairs of curved timbers that make an arch within the roof space. These arches may join on to a horizontal collar, or meet directly without the presence of a collar, rather like the two halves of a pointed-arched bridge span. The braces are supported from below by uprights called WALL-POSTS, which rest in turn on corbels that may be carved with busts, angels or grotesques. The braces too may be ornamented with moulding and carving.

The WAGON ROOF remained much in favour in the far South-West, which readily adapted the double-framed type to the ceiled, boarded or panelled form. (The principal rafters of these roofs can often be identified from below by their greater thickness and projection.) At the E end, it was customary to enhance the roof over

▲ 53. Detail of the roof of St Mary, Bettws-y-crwyn, Shropshire, c. 1500,
a late example of the use of arched braces and wind braces

the sanctuary or altar bay by means of richer carving or painting,
known as a CEILURE.

Other ways of introducing visual interest to the fabric of a roof
include the insertion of WIND BRACES. These are curved or double-
curved timbers that lie parallel with the inner surface of the roof,
between the purlins and the principal rafters. They can be deployed
in tiers of two or more, making bold patterns especially when the
curves are supplemented by cusping. These patterns were especially
popular in the West Midlands, and belong at least as much to houses
as to churches.

All these roof types may be found in churches of c14 date, or
those added at that period to older buildings. The fullest development of English church roofs belongs to the c15 and c16, and is
described on pp. 96–7.

The essential distinctions within medieval church seating follow the division between chancel and nave.

The **chancel** first. Besides any sedilia (*see* p. 50), the chancel may also have fixed wooden seats known as **stalls**. These are frequently the mark of a church that was served by a group or 'college' of priests (hence the term **collegiate church**). In their basic form these stalls follow the pattern of those of cathedrals and monastic churches, except that individual canopies are usually omitted. The stalls were customarily placed in rows facing inwards from the side walls, and continuing at right angles around the E side of the screen. The exposed end of each row may have tracery forms carved in relief. Each end is commonly carried upwards in an ogee-shaped finial ending in a fleur-de-lys or sculpted figure, a form known as a **poppyhead**. There may also be **panelling** on the stall fronts and against the side walls with delicate blind tracery for decoration, and sometimes openwork cresting along the top of the back panelling too, like that used on many screens.

The individual stalls are divided by deep, outswept arms, and each seat is hinged and tips upwards, so that the occupant could keep his place when the liturgy required him to stand. In addition, the underside of the seat has a ledge-like projection that can be used for support while standing for long periods, known as a **misericord** (from the Latin words for 'pity' and 'heart'). Very often, the lower side of the misericord is decorated with carving, from simple foliage to masks, figures, or narrative scenes that may have a humorous, even satirical character.

54. Detail of a C15 bench end of the poppyhead type, from St Mary, Withersfield, Suffolk

55. An early or mid-C15 misericord from the collegiate church of
St Laurence, Ludlow, Shropshire

Stalls are easily moved around, or transferred between churches. Some
of those now in parish churches were brought in from monastic buildings
after the Reformation. Continental examples may be found here and there
too, invariably imported in the C19 after the decimation of monastic churches
in the wake of the French Revolution. Where ensembles of medieval stalls
remain intact, they will be found to rest on a low stone wall or plinth, which
may be pierced with small openings for ventilation or (perhaps) acoustic
reasons.

For most of the Middle Ages, fixed seating for ordinary church-goers in
the **nave** was not provided. Instead, there might be a stone bench around
the inner walls of the nave, especially in large and ambitious churches. Such
benches have often been interpreted as seating for the elderly and infirm,
although they frequently lack adequate sight-lines to the altar. Movable
stools or benches may have been provided too.

From the late C14, as sermons and meditations in church became
widespread, **pews** or **benches** in the nave became more common too. Like
the stalls, they were commonly constructed as large framed installations,
each row of seating being fixed into horizontal timbers resting on the floor. In
the absence of stall divisions, canopies or wall panelling, decorative interest
was concentrated on the **bench ends** and **bench fronts**.

Medieval benches show a great deal of regional diversity. The poppyhead
type, with or without sculpted figures, is especially common in East Anglia.
In the Midlands the usual form is square-topped, with slim buttresses

▲ 56. Late medieval benches of the straight-topped kind at St John, Plymtree, Devon. The nave arcade and screen are of the same period

for ornament in imitation of stone architecture. West Country benches are typically square-topped too, but tend to be given over to deep-cut decorative carving. Relief figure scenes are widespread here, as well as vine scroll, heraldry, religious emblems, and other enduring motifs. Thanks to the regional fondness for inscribed dates, we know that the installation of benches continued in the West Country through the decades of religious upheaval and into the late C16.

As well as regional variations in design, the degree of survival also varies widely. Kent, for example, has very few intact medieval benches in its parish churches. However, bench ends may survive even when the rest is lost, having been re-fixed in new seating by Victorian restorers.

THE PERPENDICULAR STYLE: EXTERIOR

The prevailing style of English architecture changed in the C14, beginning with a few scattered instances in greater churches in the 1330s, and culminating by the end of the century in the near-universal acceptance of the new manner. Easily recognized and assimilated, the Perpendicular style ('Perp' for short) continued to be used for a great deal of church work well into the C17, long after classical and Renaissance motifs had begun to appear on furnishings and monuments (*see* p. 114).

Elements of the Perpendicular can be traced back to advanced French Gothic of the late C13, but its full realization was very much a home-grown project. Even as Continental masons developed the interlacing, double-curving motifs of the Decorated period into the bewilderingly complex Flamboyant style, English masons chose instead to straighten and simplify their architectural lines – hence the name. Many historians have been tempted to link the spread of the new manner to the shortage of skilled building workers after the Black Death (1348–9) and the epidemics that followed in its wake, but the divergence of English architecture from that of the Continent suggests that other factors must have been at work too.

The results are most conspicuous in TRACERY PATTERNS, including those of the many stone or timber surfaces decorated by blind traceried carving. Straight mullions (vertical divisions) proliferate, often making a series of upright openings known as PANEL TRACERY, in place of (or sometimes in combination with) the leaf- and net-like forms favoured in the early C14. The lines of the mullions that make the main window lights may themselves run up unbroken into the tracery, a form known as SUPER-MULLIONED. Horizontal divisions or

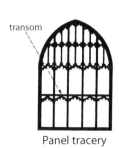

transom

Panel tracery

▲ 57. Panel-traceried windows in the Perpendicular s aisle of St Mary the Virgin, Saffron Walden, Essex. These examples are both supermullioned and supertransomed

TRANSOMS across the main window lights become more common too, and in such cases there are usually little arches to the heads of the lower lights, immediately below the transom. Transoms may also be incorporated into the tracery pattern, and these are known as SUPERTRANSOMS. A horizontal band in the tracery formed of small cusped openings is known as a LATTICED TRANSOM.

UNCUSPED ARCHES to the window lights are a late C15 development. They are understandably common in those eastern counties which took up the use of shaped and rubbed brick to make windows and simple mouldings, but they also appear in stone-building areas, so the form must have owed something to fashionable preferences as well.

The size of individual windows and the total proportion of wall space devoted to glazing continued to increase during the period, as they had done in the preceding phases of Gothic. The E window may be pushed almost to the fullest possible width, and aisles may have windows that are equal in width to the solid parts between, or wider still. Especially in larger churches, the clerestory may have its

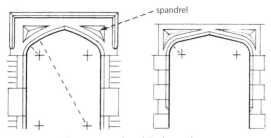

Four-centred and Tudor arches

windows doubled in number in relation to those of the aisle, leaving little more than the thickness of a buttress between each pair. As with the earlier Gothic styles, however, the dominant lines of tracery in windows with multiple lights are still often made by lesser arches. Thus a seven-light Perpendicular window will typically encompass two three-light arches, the outer sides of which are defined by the curves of the main arch.

Besides increasing in width, windows and other openings were also made larger in area by adopting the FOUR-CENTRED ARCH, which steadily supplanted the two-centred, pointed form inherited from the C14. The term TUDOR ARCH is also used, especially for the very broad and flattened four-centred forms of the later C15 and C16. Other variants include a type first used on the Divinity School at Oxford in the 1440s, in which the 'arch' is curved only at its shoulders, from which the sides continue as straight lines to a shallow triangular apex.

When used on DOORWAYS, arched heads of the period were enclosed in most cases within HOODMOULDS of rectangular shapes, thus forming two roughly triangular shapes between arch and moulding. The spaces enclosed by an arch of any shape and a

headstop -----▶

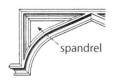

spandrel

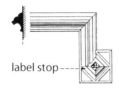

label stop

Labels

rectangular enclosure, as well as those between the individual arches of an arcade, are known as SPANDRELS. The spandrels of this type of Perpendicular doorway may be filled with foliage carving, or with the ubiquitous shields in quatrefoils.

When a hoodmould is terminated on either side of an opening, rather than running onwards as part of a continuous moulding, it is also known as a LABEL. The label or hoodmould may end in carved headstops, or in simpler mouldings known as LABEL STOPS. Diagonal or diamond-shaped label stops are an indication of a date some time after the first quarter of the C15.

A similar emphasis on straight lines influenced the treatment of other parts of the church building, large and small. Ornamental details include various forms of PANELLING, i.e. regular, straight-sided divisions of equal size. One widespread treatment from the period is a row of encircled quatrefoils within squares, sometimes with a shield or rosette in the centre. Little quatrefoils were a popular motif for friezes on plinths and parapets, including the openwork parapets favoured especially in the West Country.

Vertical accents are provided by BUTTRESSES and PINNA-CLES, characteristically combined in one tall, slim form (although buttresses that die into the walls below the parapet continued in use too). Especially after *c.* 1400, buttresses placed at outer corners are likely to stand singly at forty-five degrees rather than in right-angled pairs. This new type is known as a DIAGONAL BUTTRESS.

SPIRES fell gradually from favour, especially after the early C15; and although examples large and small continued to be built, the characteristic Perpendicular types of WEST TOWER all omit them. Regional preferences in these towers are often very pronounced. North Devon favoured a tall, straight-sided form with shallow buttresses and relatively small windows and bell-openings. In Devon and Somerset there is usually also a prominent STAIR-TURRET, placed midway along the N or S wall and rising above the battle-

▲ 58. St Peter, Tiverton, Devon, showing variety in the treatment of buttresses and panelled parapets. The s porch and chapel date from 1517

ments of the tower parapet. In London and the adjacent counties the proportions are lower and sturdier, the buttresses are more pronounced, and the stair-turret is placed at one corner, often the s e. The presence of a stone staircase may be indicated less obviously by a modest thickening of the walls or buttressing at one corner, or by the presence of little slit-like window openings at vertical intervals. East Anglian churches are more likely to fit the staircase entirely within one angle of the tower space, to allow for a symmetrical treatment of all four corners. Where no staircase can be detected within the walls of the tower, wooden stairs or internal ladders were (and often still are) used for access to the upper stages.

The most demonstrative towers are found in less turbulent regions, in places where good building stone was abundant. Somerset is especially well favoured, and its Perpendicular towers include some of the most lavish and inventive anywhere. Sometimes their buttresses and pinnacles surge up to the corners of the parapet; sometimes they die into the tower just below, leaving the parapet and corner pinnacles to be corbelled outwards from the upper walls. Parapets may be pierced in superimposed tiers, sometimes in the form of openwork battlements (which are used on the rest of the church too), and small sculpted figures are common. Window openings are repeated and sometimes multiplied as the stages rise, or are vertically linked through the storeys; belfry openings are filled with decorative pierced stonework, alias SOMERSET TRACERY, rather than the angled slats favoured elsewhere.

Even in areas of more limited architectural ambition, a grand urban church tower might still achieve something spectacular. One unforgettable example is the so-called flying steeple at St Nicholas, Newcastle upon Tyne (now Cathedral), in which four big flying buttresses curve inwards from the corner pinnacles to support a tall stone lantern which is topped with its own slim spirelet, and set about with gilded weathervanes.

Where good building stone was not easily to be had, masons could make inventive use of what was to hand, as long as there was money for building. In the flinty areas of East Anglia, Norfolk especially, this encouraged the use of FLUSHWORK. The term refers to the insertion of lighter-coloured stone into surfaces faced with flints that have been broken or KNAPPED to make a smooth surface. The usual motifs mimic the outlines of basic ornamental forms such as panelling and quatrefoils, but more ambitious effects

59. The Somerset church of St Mary, Bruton, C15 and early C16. The W tower is of the regional type with a stair-turret at one corner and pierced stone openings in the upper stages. Typical Perpendicular features include the large clerestorey and W window and the W doorway with its square hood-mould, but the assertive porch-tower to the N aisle is very unusual

▲ 60. The s porch of St Mary, Kersey, Suffolk, a good example of East Anglian flushwork from the C15

61. St Leonard, Middleton, Lancashire, illustrates the long and low proportions favoured in the North West in the C15 and C16. The timber belfry is C17

were sometimes achieved too. Spectacular, stencil-like architectural patterns of knapped flint clothe much of St Michael Coslany in Norwich, and Long Melford church (Suffolk) has a lengthy series of flushwork inscriptions from the 1480s that tell of its rebuilding.

In the absence of such helpful pointers, Perpendicular work can be difficult to date from appearance alone. This is partly because the style held sway over such a long period, but also because many master masons appear to have adopted new forms without entirely discarding older ones. For example, the individual lights of a window are more likely to have ogee- or two-centred-arched heads at the start of the period than at its end, by which time four-centred-arched heads had become common, but both of the older forms remained common currency during the C15.

8 PERPENDICULAR CHURCH INTERIORS

ARCADES of the later Perpendicular period may incorporate the four-centred-arched form, as in the double-aisled church of St Helen at Abingdon (Berks., now Oxon). However, the structurally stronger two-centred form continued in use too. Also taken over from earlier centuries were simple octagonal piers and the double chamfering of the arcade arches. As a result, many ordinary Perpendicular arcades do not look very different from those of the C13.

PIERS often display continuity too, including the standard London type of quatrefoil section with four slim shafts. More complex forms of pier show greater innovation. Especially distinctive is the elongated, lozenge-shaped form that appeared in East Anglia in the mid C14, which was aligned with its narrower sides towards nave and aisle in order to maximize the visible width of the openings. Generally. arches may rest on round, polygonal or clustered shafts, each with its own cap. The diagonal pier faces between may be treated with wave, sunk or hollow mouldings, or simply left flat. Rather than stopping at the level of the capitals, these diagonals run unbroken around the arch (a device already widespread in the C14).

CAPITALS may be carved with thick and dense foliage or angel busts, and are sometimes topped with miniature crenellations. Their basic form is usually polygonal, a shape stressed by the ABACUS or top member. In Devon and Somerset especially, there may be band-like carved capitals that embrace all sides of the pier, thus interrupting the diagonal mouldings between pier and arch. Many of these details develop themes already present in Decorated work.

BASES of the period are characteristically polygonal too, and follow the outlines of the attached shafts. They are also considerably taller than the flat, floor-hugging bases of Norman and early Gothic times. This extra height allows for some complex architectural interplay in cases where each shaft is given its own miniature base that merges below into the main, shared one.

62. The nave interior of the double-aisled church of St Helen, Abingdon, Oxfordshire (formerly Berkshire), showing both two-centred and four-centred arches. Some of the piers are of an uncommon concave-sided section

63. A late Perpendicular foliage capital of West Country type, from St Peter and St Paul, Churchstanton, Somerset

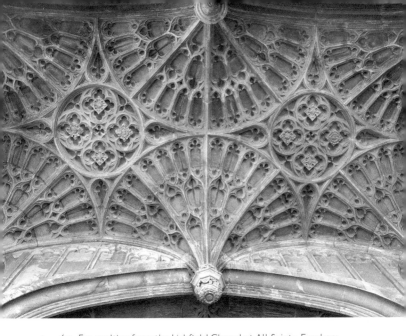

As already noted, VAULTING of the main spaces of a parish church remained exceptionally rare; but the characteristic form of English late Gothic, the FAN VAULT, may appear in porches, chapels and other subsidiary spaces. Fan vaults consist of tapering conoid shapes rather than intersecting arched volumes, and are constructed not of separate ribs infilled with thin cells of stone, but of curved stone panels on which the dense pattern of ribs and ornament is carved in relief. The fully vaulted church at Ottery St Mary church in Devon includes a fan vault over one outer aisle, added as a private chapel some time after c. 1504, and there is another fan-vaulted aisle at Cullompton church in the same county. In both cases the bosses are elongated into PENDANTS, an embellishment typical of fan vaults.

Some unusually ambitious parish churches, especially those in towns or in villages made prosperous by the wool and cloth trades, adopted coherent INTERNAL ELEVATIONS, like those of cathedrals and grand monastic churches. That is to say, the walls of the central space and of the inner walls of the aisles are treated as coherent architectural designs, tying together the arcades, windows and roof supports into a single system of vertical and horizontal mouldings. In this type of interior, wall-shafts typically run upwards through the clerestory from the centre of each pier (with or without a break at capital level), and sometimes also from the apex of each arch. Each shaft can thus end in a corbel supporting a wall-post of the roof, a treatment which may also extend to the walls and roofs of the aisles. Above the main arcade, the wall surface below and around the clerestory windows may in the richest cases be treated with all-over panelling. An early example of this system is the nave at Burwell in Cambridgeshire, from the third quarter of the C15. A contrasting late medieval type, of which the late C14 Norfolk church of North Walsham is an early representative, has neither chancel arch nor clerestory. Here the arcades run through from end to end,

65. The nave of St Mary, Burwell, Cambridgeshire, built c. 1454–77. An early instance of the design of the arcades and clerestory of a parish church as one consistent internal elevation. The piers are of the diagonal type originating in East Anglia, the roof is of shallow arch-braced form with traceried openings above the arches

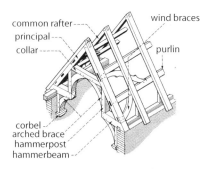

common rafter
principal
collar
wind braces
purlin
corbel
arched brace
hammerpost
hammerbeam

Hammerbeam roof

and the wall space above them is minimized.

Ambitious churches like these may come with one of the spectacular ROOFS with which late medieval master carpenters liked to cover the nave. The best-known type is the HAM-MERBEAM ROOF, which was widely taken up in East Anglian and Lincolnshire churches after its first use at the royal Westminster Hall in the late C14. The design achieves exceptionally broad spans by supporting its arched braces on pairs of beams projecting horizontally from the wall. The arched braces do not join directly on to these hammerbeams, but are attached to HAMMERPOSTS that are set vertically at the end of each beam. Each hammerbeam is supported in turn by its own arched brace and wall-post.

Hammerbeam trusses may also be used selectively, alternating with simple tie-beam trusses or arched braces. At the opposite extreme, the system can be amplified by means of an upper tier of arched braces, with or without hammerposts, making a DOUBLE HAMMERBEAM ROOF. Roofs with upper hammerposts include Gestingthorpe in Essex; those without include St Wendreda's church at March (Cambs.), where each tier of hammerbeams ends in broad-winged angels holding religious emblems.

Rows of carved angels may also decorate the wall-plates of late medieval church roofs of every type. A favourite roof form in western and south-western counties has broad KINGPOST TRUSSES which are elaborated by means of mullions, open timber tracery or figured fretwork in the triangular gap between each tie-beam and the rafters above it. In the intervals between the principal rafters, the roof surface is made into a panelled grid by means of moulded

66. The double hammerbeam roof of the nave of St Mary, Gestingthorpe, Essex, of c. 1525

purlins and the lesser rafters, and this grid can be elaborated further with bosses and tracery. A more modest version of this treatment may be found over aisles that have roofs of the gabled and double-pitched kind. Here the space available for a display of openwork above the tie-beam is smaller, or (in a shallow-pitched roof) absent altogether. Thus the lower surface of the roof acquires the character of a timbered ceiling. Single-pitched aisle roofs can likewise make do with the panelled rafter-and-purlin treatment alone.

The increasing shallowness of average ROOF PITCHES in this period owed much to a change in materials: costly but durable lead replaced tiles or the thin slabs known as stone slates as the outer covering.

Medieval parish churches were thickly populated with images. Carvings of one kind or another could be applied to almost any structural part or furnishing, from fine statues to rough grotesques. Altars also displayed panel paintings or **reredoses**, of which a bare handful survive. Reredoses carved from stone or wood were popular too, and the stone type has lasted a little better, although any remaining sculpted figures are now usually heavily defaced within their architectural setting.

Churches may also display the sculpted **alabaster panels** that were mass-produced especially in Nottinghamshire and Derbyshire from the late C14 onwards. Easily transportable, and popular with private patrons and foreign markets, many of these panels escaped the purges of religious imagery that followed the Reformation. Some of these survivors have since found their way into churches to which they did not originally belong.

In addition, churches were liberally decorated with **two-dimensional imagery**, such as the figures of saints painted on the front panels of some screens (*see* p. 52). The most abundant and ambitious categories are wall painting and stained glass.

Wall paintings have often been inadvertently protected under whitewash or plaster, so that fresh examples are still being uncovered. However, paintings are also prone to fade or flake away once exposed to light and air, and some recorded by earlier generations are now scarcely visible. Despite these losses, hundreds of wall paintings survive: enough to give a reasonable idea of the prevalent styles and subjects.

The earliest painted schemes that are still near-complete date from the C12; Essex, Kent and Sussex are among the best hunting places. As church

▼   67. The stone reredos of c. 1400 at St Paul, Hammoon, Dorset, a rare
undefaced example

68. The painted apse of St Michael and All Angels. Copford, Essex, of c. 1125–30, partly renewed in 1871–2

69. Two popular subjects painted in the C15 in St Breaca, Breage, Cornwall: St Christopher, left, and the 'Sunday Christ', shown with the implements used by Sabbath-breakers that have wounded his body

windows were then still relatively few and small, it was easy to display long narrative sequences in tiers on the N and S walls, not always extending as far as the W end. The vaulted apse of Copford church (Essex) has a theologically coherent sequence of C12 paintings, partly renewed in the Victorian restoration, that continue across the arch and on to the walls of chancel and nave. Where paintings survive in quantity, however, it is more usual to find a mixture of scenes of different periods, sometimes overlaid on one another.

As to **imagery**, a Last Judgment was commonly applied to the wall above and around the chancel arch, sometimes with the Damned and the Saved depicted on opposing sides. Another common subject was a giant St Christopher bearing the Christ Child through the waters, usually placed on the wall confronting the main entrance. Christopher was the patron saint of travellers, and it was believed that anyone who saw his image would be protected from death on that day.

Other saints may appear as single figures holding or wearing their identifying attributes, or in narrative scenes, such as the combat between St George and the dragon or the many legends of the Life of the Virgin. Moralizing imagery of other kinds was common too, especially from the C14 onwards: the Acts of Mercy, the Seven Deadly Sins, the Wheel of Fortune, the Archangel Michael weighing souls in the balance, or the group known as the Three Living and the Three Dead. Images of Christ's wounded body conveyed explicit warnings against swearing or breaking the Sabbath (in which everyday working implements are shown to have caused the injuries). The perils of gossip were signalled by the devil Titivillus, shown with his scroll for noting down idle or malicious words.

Much medieval wall painting was much simpler, consisting of **simple patterns**, or imitations of more prestigious materials. Painted wall-hangings may appear, and in the C13 and C14 a schematized version of ashlar masonry, represented by 'stoning' in patterns suggesting the joints of rectangular blocks, often with rosettes or the letter 'M' (for Mary) in the middle of each block. These may underlie later pictorial work, which in turn may have been obscured by the **texts** stipulated by the newly Protestant church authorities after the Reformation. Simple inscriptions may accompany medieval images too, usually in Latin rather than English.

Medieval **stained glass** likewise tends to survive only in a damaged or fragmentary state. Sometimes what bits and pieces remain have been gathered together and re-set in a single panel, collage-fashion. *In situ* glass may be limited to the tracery, the major images in the main lights having been

▲ 70. Early C14 stained glass from St John the Baptist, Cockayne Hatley, Bedfordshire. The deep colours and the composition of single figures in architectural surrounds are typical of the period

lost. On the other hand, the medium is more durable than wall painting, and what is left may give a better idea of how a window originally appeared.

Glazing of any kind was costly, and most early churches made do with wooden shutters, framed parchment or oiled linen in their windows. The oldest stained glass remaining in English parish churches belongs to the late C12 and C13, and is not plentiful. This early glass depended on the use of separate, single-coloured pieces on which outlines such as features and drapery were applied, all held within a matrix of lead strips defining the main lines of the composition. Figures are typically portrayed singly, and any narrative scenes are framed in medallion or vesica shapes. Colours are dark and rich, but lighter effects may be created by means of grey-stained geometrical and foliage patterns, known as **grisaille**. Shields with heraldic decoration began to appear here and there in the second half of the C13, becoming a key component of English stained glass within a few generations.

Narrative scenes became more common in the C14. At the same time the glass itself was made thinner. After c. 1310 it was sometimes also coloured with the yellow pigment known as **silver stain**, which could be applied selectively on a single piece of glass. Colours in general became lighter in the C14, and the dark flesh tones of much C13 work were no longer used.

C14 glaziers enhanced the lighter effects achievable in silver-stain glass by combining figures or narrative scenes in horizontal zones with large areas of grisaille or clear ('white') glass above and below, a composition known as a **band window**. Another C14 development was the framing of individual figures within images of architectural canopies, with or without the suggestion of false perspective. Towards the end of the C14, large grisaille patterns declined in favour of assemblages of the individually patterned but standard-sized pieces known as **quarries**. Darker tones were used in tracery lights, including the twisting dagger and mouchette shapes in which glaziers showed off their ingenuity in combining figures, emblems and patterns.

Perpendicular panel tracery allowed a more orderly treatment of the glazing, in which rows of similar figures – saints and angels in particular – readily found a place, as well as heraldic shields. Similar **figure rows** on a larger scale were a common choice for the main lights, framed in architectural canopy work. By the C15 inscriptions adopted the strongly vertical Gothic form known as **blackletter**, and colours became softer and less intense, with greater boldness in the use of white glass.

The unravelling of England's native tradition of glass-making was already in progress before the Reformation, chiefly on account of an influx of

▲　71. A detail of the E window of St Andrew, Greystoke, Cumbria (formerly Westmorland), probably of the late C15. The high proportion of white glass and the use of pale yellow silver-stain pigment place the work in the later Middle Ages

craftsmen and imports from the Low Countries. The new school of glass-making depended much less on lead work or on architectural canopies for making compositions. Its products came in large sheets painted with a broader range of enamelled colours, and showed an enthusiasm for **pictorial effects** such as landscape or townscape backgrounds, comparable to those of panel paintings. An early stage in this movement is captured at Fairford in Gloucestershire, the only English parish church to retain a complete medieval glazing scheme. The glass here dates from the early C16, and is attributed to the workshop of the King's Glazier, the Flemish glass-stainer Barnard Flower.

More common in churches than windows of this late type are the silver-stained or enamelled **roundels** and small panels made in northern Europe in the C16 and C17. It is not always possible to discover how and when these easily transported pieces found their way into English church windows.

Medieval **floor tiles** may be decorated with simple but vivid light-on-dark outlines of figures or animals, as well as heraldry, foliage and simpler patterns. The most ambitious images may extend over several tiles, but parish churches are more likely to have self-contained, single designs, usually re-laid out of their original context.

9 THE IMPACT OF THE REFORMATION

Beginning in the 1530s under Henry VIII, the Church of England was transformed into a Protestant body, with the monarch rather than the pope as its supreme head. The consequences for parish life and church buildings were drastic. Prayers for the dead were abolished, cutting off in full flood the life of the guilds and chantries and making their chapels redundant. Prayers addressed through saints were done away with too, and most religious imagery fell into disfavour. Cult statues were destroyed and the great sculpted or painted Crucifixion groups over the rood screen were taken down. Especially vulnerable were representations of St Mary the Virgin and of St Thomas à Becket, a popular saint who was associated with the independence of the Church from royal power. Instead, texts prevailed over images: a bible was ordered to be placed in every church, the Ten Commandments and Creed had to be painted at the altar end, and painted scriptural texts obliterated religious imagery on the walls. Services henceforth were in English rather than Latin, and conducted by clergy who were now free to marry.

By the standards of some Continental countries, the English Reformation was nevertheless relatively gentle. Images were purged in an orderly fashion, without the surges of popular iconoclasm of the kind that sacked churches in the Netherlands. Twists and turns in royal policy, including the return to Roman Catholic allegiance and imagery in the 1550s under Queen Mary and the conscious avoidance of unnecessary confrontation by her successor, Queen Elizabeth, appear in many parishes to have encouraged a cautious, wait-and-see attitude to church furnishings and liturgy.

It was also both impracticable and costly to eliminate imagery completely. The replacement of so much stained glass with plain was expensive, and might be deferred; effigies on tombs and monuments were allowed to remain, and often some of the lesser sculpture too; carved angels, headstops and grotesques could be difficult to reach, and were not necessarily offensive to Protestant beliefs in any case.

The loss of medieval religious art is best understood instead as a long process of which the C16 Reformation was only the first instalment. Fresh programmes of iconoclasm were launched in the 1640s–50s during the Civil War and Commonwealth; the journals of the zealous William Dowsing during this period give a detailed, church-by-church account of his team of deputies' progress through East Anglia, hunting down and 'cleansing' anything suggestive of Catholic belief and practice. But a great deal that survived such assaults gradually disappeared in later centuries, by accident or neglect more than by ideological attack. At a time when few people were interested in the material remains of the past, it was not easy to justify the cost of restoring (say) damaged and draughty stained glass rather than installing plain new windows, or planning new church seating in such a way that an inconveniently placed medieval monument or screen could be retained. As writings and records by early antiquaries and topographers show, a great deal of old work that survived into the late C17 and C18 disappeared quietly under the generations that followed.

72. St Mary, Ellingham, Hampshire, showing C17 painted texts in place of the medieval crucifixion group on the tympanum over the chancel screen. The family pew (left) and pulpit are also C17

PULPIT AND ALTAR

Preaching was increasingly part of the activities of the late medieval church, and fixed **pulpits** were already present in a good many churches by the early C16. Around sixty **stone pulpits** survive from before the Reformation, including concentrations in Gloucestershire, Somerset and Devon. Many are built integrally with an arcade pier or respond, including the unusually lavish example at St Peter, Wolverhampton (Staffs.). Others stand against a wall, and are approached by stairs within the wall thickness, as at Hutton in Somerset. Both types commonly feature a slim supporting shaft placed against pier or wall, from which the pulpit is corbelled out. The usual form is octagonal, and the sides are invariably treated with architectural motifs such as niches and blind panel tracery.

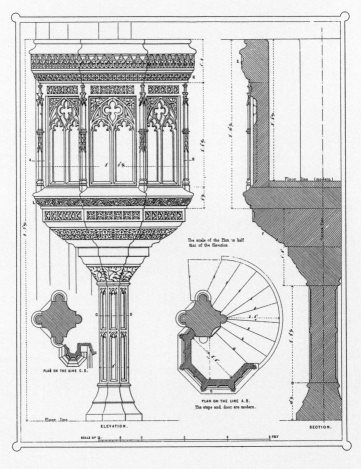

Just under a hundred **wooden pulpits** remain from the Middle Ages, although quite a few have been heavily reconstructed and almost all lack their original steps. Most are octagonal, but hexagonal or part-hexagonal shapes also appear, and in greater numbers than for stone pulpits. Norfolk (the best county for painted figures) and Devon top the list, with good showings also from Somerset and Cambridgeshire.

As well as architectural motifs, some West Country wooden pulpits adopt the thick foliage and figurative carving seen on screens and bench ends and in the same region (*see* pp. 52 and 81). Wood being lighter than stone, the base may curve inwards to a single supporting post, as with a good many in Cambridgeshire and Suffolk (the 'wine-glass' type). A few specimens

73. Stone pulpit of late medieval type from St Andrew, Banwell, Somerset, engraved in 1849

74. Wooden pulpit of c. 1498 from St John the Baptist, Stoke-by-Clare, Suffolk

▲ 75. Pulpit and tester of 1631 from St Thomas, Newport, Isle of Wight. The stairs are later

survive of pulpits hewn from a single piece of oak, including a hexagonal one at Mellor in Cheshire.

Although the Reformation replaced Latin services with English, the government sought to control what was said in church by licensing a limited number of approved preachers. As a result there was little immediate demand for new pulpits, and far fewer datable Elizabethan examples exist than medieval ones. From this time onwards pulpits were almost always made of wood.

The early C17 was a more favourable time for preaching, and 'Jacobean' pulpits (often from Charles I's reign, after 1625, rather than from James I's) are quite common. Characteristic decoration includes round-arched classical arcading, the Flemish-derived decoration like bands of cut leather known as **strapwork**, and other mouldings from the Renaissance repertoire.

Pulpits of the period may also be crowned by a broad sounding-board or **tester**, for which little pendants at the angles are the favourite embellishment. Sometimes the tester has an ogee-shaped wooden dome on top. It may also have a supporting back-board. C17 and C18 **hour glasses** for timing sermons survive here and there, with their wrought-iron supports.

Pulpits made after the Restoration of 1660 were likely to follow the lead set by new London churches, including those rebuilt after the Great Fire of 1666. Wreaths, swags, cherub-heads and other deep-cut carving replaced the shallower Jacobean forms, and more use was made of inlaid marquetry patterns. The staircase may have elegant balusters and open-sided treads, like those of private houses.

Lecterns are stands for service books or bibles. They have angled tops, and are commonly free-standing. The most familiar type in English churches takes the form of an eagle with outspread wings, standing on a globe. The base or feet may rest on little lions. Most of these are Victorian or C20 versions of a widespread late medieval type, of which some fifty have survived in parish churches. Like the originals, the later versions may be of brass or of carved wood. The traditional eagle type was perpetuated here and there in the C17 and C18.

Other lecterns have simple sloping tops, which are sometimes placed back-to-back. Medieval examples tend to have ornament derived from architecture, such as buttresses to the support. An especially beautiful wooden example from the C14 is at Detling in Kent, with a top that exceptionally slopes back on all four sides. There are also a few **stone lecterns** built into the chancel wall. Derbyshire has the largest cluster, including a castellated one at Chaddesden.

Especially in the C18, the functions of pulpit and lectern were often combined with the desk of the parish clerk in a **three-decker pulpit**. Unpopular with Victorian restorers, these impressive structures survive intact mostly in churches which have also kept their full complement of Georgian seating. Rarer still, but once relatively common, are churches in which the pulpit stands directly on the central axis, blocking views of the chancel and altar. Whitby church in Yorkshire (North Riding) is the best-known example.

76. An intact three-decker pulpit of c. 1750, from All Saints, Cottesbrooke, Northampton-shire

Victorian pulpits by contrast are almost always separate furnishings. Stone returned to fashion at this time, especially for those pulpits which echo medieval Italian methods of inlaid coloured marble.

Altars show much less continuity with the medieval church. Before the Reformation, altars were mostly fixtures of stone. These were almost all destroyed in favour of **communion tables** of wood, as ordered in 1550. The change reflected the Protestant interpretation of communion as a purely commemorative service, rather than the miraculous re-enactment of the Catholic Mass, by which wine and bread are transformed into the blood and body of Christ.

Side altars and private chapels having been suppressed, most churches needed only one such table. It was initially placed end-on in the chancel, some way short of the E wall, so that the congregation could gather round on all sides. These solid and substantial tables do not necessarily differ from ordinary domestic work of the period, which is not to say that they are always plain; the legs in particular may be turned, with big bulbous projections, and the vertical faces may have shallow carved decoration.

C17 and C18 examples also follow domestic fashions, sometimes including the presence of marble tops. The main change during this period concerned the setting of the communion table within the chancel. In the 1630s under Archbishop Laud, the authorities tried to enforce a position flat against the E wall, as in the medieval period. The rule was revived at the Restoration, and became standard Anglican practice until recent times.

Communion rails were also installed after the Reformation to define and protect the area around the table, thus sparing it from the disrespectful attentions of dogs. The rails also served as a place for the congregation to kneel when taking communion. Some run straight across the chancel; others make a three-sided enclosure around the table. A few churches, including Lyddington in Rutland (dated 1635), still have four-sided enclosures, allowing originally for communicants to kneel on the E side as well. Also worth mention is Deerhurst in Gloucestershire, both for its early communion rails and because the chancel walls still have all-round fixed seating of the early C17, including across the E wall.

Communion rails became a favourite means of display for craftsmanship in the C17 and C18. The simplest had turned balusters like those used for staircases, with a development from vertically symmetrical to bellied or bottle-shaped forms during the C17. A few surviving early C17 sets use spiky interrupted shapes, arranged like stalactites and stalagmites; some post-Restoration rails are treated as swirling openwork panels of carved foliage. Decorative wrought-iron rails were a fashion of the early C18, when the repertoire of wooden forms extended to include tall and slim balusters that may be straight, spiral or twisted in shape. Cast iron was sometimes used in the early C19, but the later Gothic Revival more often looked to the forms of medieval wrought ironwork when making communion rails.

The C17 return of the altar to the E end encouraged the development of the **reredos**, typically as a wooden installation in which classical pilasters or columns framed the mandatory painted texts of Commandments, Creed and Lord's Prayer. This is another feature for which the London City churches of the years after 1666 appear to have provided influential models. Flaming urns were a popular choice as ornaments on the top. Most of the City churches also adopted the C17 fashion for **black and white paving** around the altar, and this continued into the early C19.

Religious **imagery** also reappeared within some C17 reredoses, including the figures of Moses and Aaron (representing kingship and priesthood), as well as the ubiquitous cherub-heads and the occasional angel. Angels and cherub-heads were also considered acceptable subjects for painted ceilings. Encouraged by the élite taste for Italian art, C18 parishes were more accommodating to religious imagery, including painted altarpieces. (It is no coincidence that many college chapels at Oxford and Cambridge, where

a high proportion of clergy were educated, acquired altarpieces during the late C17 and C18.) There are even a few church interiors with schemes of Baroque wall painting, including Little Stanmore in Middlesex (now London), a benefaction of the Duke of Chandos from c. 1720.

Installations like these fell into disfavour after the 1830s, especially in medieval churches. Instead, Victorian taste often preferred a display of polished marble as a backing for the altar, sometimes with imagery sculpted in wood or stone, sometimes with painted or mosaic scenes. Many 'Low Church' parishes continued to frown on the use of art in religious contexts, however, and relied on texts or symbols to ornament the E end. The growing popularity of ornamented **frontals** of embroidered cloth discouraged any decoration of the altar table itself.

10 CHURCH BUILDINGS FROM THE REFORMATION TO c. 1660

The consequences of the Reformation for architecture are not always easy to assess. Religious uncertainties were the enemy of initiative, and very few wholly new churches date from the second half of the c16. However, projects already in progress could be brought quietly to a conclusion even after the break with Rome. Fire, structural collapse and other mishaps to church buildings also had to be made good. The development of change-ringing in the c16–c17 was an incentive to repair or rebuild church towers. Family chapels continued to be built or rebuilt too, even though they were no longer used for private Masses.

During this period there was no perception that Perpendicular Gothic was an improper style for churches, or that pointed arches conflicted with Protestantism. Early classical or 'Antique' architectural forms of Renaissance derivation (*see also* pp. 108 and 122) had already appeared in England a generation before the English Reformation, but never displaced the medieval manner entirely. The association between churches and Gothic architecture remained exceptionally strong, and the style seemed right and proper for the purpose even as classical forms began to dominate monuments and fittings. Likewise, chapels in some great Jacobean country houses were distinguished by having Perpendicular traceried windows, while the colleges of Oxford and Cambridge commissioned very little entirely classical architecture before 1660. As the fanciful and poetic silhouettes of many Elizabethan and Jacobean great houses suggest, the Gothic style also benefited more generally from its chivalric or romantic associations.

This conservatism in matters of style can make church work of the later c16 and early c17 hard to identify. Yet we know from dated examples that the native tradition was still resilient enough to produce some convincing late Gothic churches even a century or more after the Reformation. Low Ham church in Somerset, built as

▲ 79. Holy Trinity, Staunton Harold, Leicestershire, 1653–65, from the E

a private chapel around 1620, and most aspects of Staunton Harold church in Leicestershire, begun as late in 1653 on his own land by the imprisoned Royalist Sir Robert Shirley, are close enough to the conventions of two hundred years before to deceive all but a close inspection.

One tell-tale in these post-Reformation Gothic churches is a tendency to hark back to early styles of tracery. At Staunton Harold the aisles and E window use cusped intersecting tracery suggestive of the early C14. At Low Ham the tracery is of standardized Perpendicular panel form except in the E window, which introduces a rose-like circle with thorny cusping, reminiscent of advanced Bristol work from the same period. Another example is the E window of St Katharine Cree in the City of London, largely rebuilt in 1628–31. The source of its rose-in-square design is the late C13 E window of Old St Paul's Cathedral, lost in the Great Fire of 1666.

St Katharine Cree combines explicitly Gothic windows with a spidery, near-flat plaster rib vault that evokes medieval forms only loosely. By contrast, the rest of the interior architecture is markedly classical: round-arched arcades spring from Corinthian COLUMNS, and a moulded CORNICE runs horizontally along the tops of the arches, from which pilasters with classical capitals extend up to the ceiling. Similar instances of hybridity include Standish church in

Lancashire, which was largely rebuilt in the 1580s. Here the arcade columns are treated like fat, straight-sided versions of the classical Tuscan order, complete with square bases and square abaci. The 1630s church of St John at Leeds has arcade piers of something like the familiar octagonal section, but the capitals are ornamented with a free combination of classical mouldings. As it happens, the windows at this church are another instance of using Perpendicular forms along the sides and showy, flowing Decorated tracery motifs at the E end. Together, these three examples suggest that the Perpendicular traditions held up better for external than for internal architecture.

A handful of explicitly CLASSICAL parish church buildings date from before the Civil Wars of the 1640s. The royal architect Inigo Jones's St Paul Covent Garden (1631–5) is the best survivor in London, allowing for its reconstruction in the 1790s following a destructive fire. An immensely sophisticated exercise in architectural primitivism,

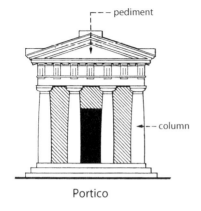

Portico

it attempted a modern version of a Tuscan (or Etruscan) temple, complete with a full-width P O R - T I C O composed of columns, arched side walls, and a triangular P E D I M E N T.

As completed, St Paul's church had an altar at the E end in the traditional way (the portico on the E wall, facing the piazza, is not in fact the main entrance, but an adjunct to the altar wall). Jones had wanted the altar at the W end, but the bishop would not allow it. Less conventional is the treatment of the interior as a single space, without a separate chancel. This was better suited for Protestant services, in which the emphasis was placed on reading and preaching rather than ritual. Another innovation was the broad, flat ceiling, made possible by an advanced form of kingpost truss which Jones derived from his knowledge of buildings in Italy. The new form signalled the eclipse of the open roof in English church architecture.

Those who wished to dispense with liturgical worship altogether had the upper hand during the Commonwealth of the 1650s, when

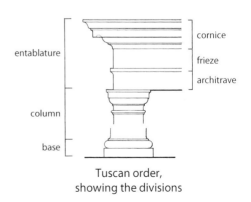

Tuscan order,
showing the divisions

82. St Matthias, Poplar, London, 1652–4, interior

the Church of England was officially (if temporarily) abolished, along with its monarchical head and hierarchy of bishops. Churches from this decade are therefore few. St Matthias, Poplar (East London), built in 1652–4 to an aisled plan chosen in the 1630s, is especially interesting because it breaks with the convention of straight arcades marching uniformly up the nave. Instead, eight big Tuscan-type columns are spaced so as to support a straight ENTABLATURE (the term used for the combination of a classical cornice with two lower members, the FRIEZE and ARCHITRAVE). This is broken where a transverse barrel vault of plaster crosses the church, intersecting the barrel vault of the nave's central vessel. The four corner areas defined by this cross-shaped vaulting are given flat ceilings, and the church in its C17 form was without a structurally separate chancel.

Although its exterior originally had some quasi-Gothic features, the plan at St Matthias is explicitly of a Protestant type, with parallels in recent Netherlandish church architecture. It thus points forward to the resurgence in classical church building after the Restoration of 1660, and especially to the restocking of the City of London with churches after the Great Fire of 1666 (*see* p. 130).

All the churches singled out above are showpieces of their period, and as such are exceptional in national terms. Most Elizabethan and early to mid-C17 architectural work is not nearly so ambitious or distinctive. It may betray its origin by obvious differences from medieval work alongside, such as the adoption of brick, the use of a rounded rather than a pointed arch, the stepping of the heads of three-light windows, or merely by a degree of coarseness, flatness or lumpiness in the mouldings. Certain absences can also be telling: window lights with plain straight heads rather than arches, arched lights without cusping (although these may also be late medieval), doorways without the familiar quatrefoils in the spandrels. Another alteration that may date from any time up to the early C19 is a plain window inserted high up in the wall towards the E end of the nave, which served to throw more light on the pulpit.

More often than in the late Middle Ages, church work may also display a carved or painted year date. In some contexts such dates must be approached with caution, as they may refer to repairs, such as the replacement of selected timbers in an existing roof. But if a porch looks post-medieval and bears a late C16 or C17 date, it is probably the real thing.

83. The tower of All Saints, Crondall, Hampshire, as rebuilt in brick c. 1659. Proportions, profile and buttresses are still of late medieval type, but the details are mostly classical

POST-REFORMATION CHURCH MONUMENTS

The English Reformation fostered an upsurge in the size and ambition of **church monuments**. Churches which had been under monastic patronage were now subject to laymen, who took over the historic responsibility to maintain the chancel. In parishes where the new patrons invoked the right of burial, a growing number of chancels took on the character of family mausolea. Similarly, the now altar-less private chapels of wealthy families could be given over to dynastic collections of monuments, private pews (*see* p. 140), or a combination of the two.

The range of monument types also expanded. **Standing monuments** that rested on the floor were joined by new varieties of **wall** or **hanging monuments**. The smallest and plainest of these, usually based on an oblong shape, are often called **tablets**. Such monuments were affordable across an increasingly broad social range, and in many churches the late C18 and early C19 contingents outnumber those of all earlier periods combined. Sometimes a wall monument also has a corresponding **ledger slab**, a big grave marker set into the church floor. Black marble was the favoured material for these slabs, which may be beautifully carved with heraldry and inscriptions. Less durable are the painted and lettered **wooden monuments** that served as a cheap alternative to stone, and which are now effectively extinct in many counties. At the other end of the scale, advanced architectural tastes interacted with the output of almost every significant sculptor active during the period. So the story of post-Reformation English church monuments is long and complex, and there is room here for only a brief outline.

Most **Elizabethan and early C17 monuments** can be read as translations of pre-Reformation types into classical language, often supplied by immigrant Flemish craftsmen, or as imitations of their work. Recumbent effigies remained common, placed on tomb-chests that now might have columns, pilasters or balusters on the sides in place of quatrefoils or panel tracery. The graceful trailing forms known as **ribbonwork** appear by way of ornament, joined after c. 1580 by the thicker, leather-like forms of **strapwork**. Sculpted **trophies of arms** may be shown in relief too, a device that was extended in later generations to include civilian objects suggestive of a trade or profession. The convention of little mourning figures continued, usually rendered as kneeling children or kinfolk. As well as on the tomb-chest, these may appear against the back wall, framed by the canopy. More economical forms include the slate tombs of Cornwall, in which the effigy is carved in shallow relief, and the continuing (but never widespread) tradition of incised pictorial outlines.

▲ 84. A typical grand late Elizabethan standing monument, to Thomas Smythe (d. 1591), at St Mary, Ashford, Kent

◁ 85. Nicholas Stone's monument to St Thomas and Lady Merry, 1633, at St Mary, Walthamstow, Greater London. The oval niches, broken-pedimented top and use of black and white marble all represent the new fashions of the mid C17

▷ 86. An early C18 cartouche from St Cuthbert, Churchtown, Lancashire, to Thomas Fleetwood (d. 1717)

Arched and flat-topped canopies were both current, often combined so that the arch is framed by side columns supporting a straight entablature. The top frequently has a lively silhouette made up variously of obelisks, cresting, heraldry or sculpted figures. Free-standing canopied monuments were also set up. They may treat the arch as a tunnel vault running right through, or surround the tomb-chest with a palisade of columns that stand directly on the floor. Both free-standing and wall-backed monuments may be guarded by iron **railings**, a common protective measure for monuments from the Middle Ages to the early C17.

Prone figures with hands clasped in prayer remained common, but other Elizabethan subjects are represented as if in life. Recumbent figures may prop their heads on one elbow, turning towards the viewer. **Kneeling figures** of less than life-size are also widespread, especially on wall monuments; one much-used formula shows husband and wife together, each with a prayer desk (prie-dieu). Another late C16 innovation was the depiction of frontal **half-length figures**, a format initially favoured for clergy and scholars in particular.

Colour was essential to the effect of most Elizabethan and Jacobean monuments. Alabaster remained in favour for the best effigies, with paint or gilding deployed on costumes and other details. Columns were often painted with marble patterns, or were themselves of black marble. Restorers sometimes try to re-create these applied colourings, not always successfully.

Many aspects of taste in monuments changed in the **early c17**, especially from c. 1620. There is a new freedom in representing the subjects, who may be shown standing or seated, often with allegorical figures represented to a smaller scale. Where effigies are still recumbent they are given a more upright and alert posture, and no longer rest head on hand. A less long-lived innovation was to represent figures in their shrouds, as if alive and resurrected on the Last Day. As a variant on the half-length format, true **portrait busts** were sometimes preferred, i.e. showing head and shoulders only, in the Roman fashion. Around 1640 a new form of hanging monument appeared, the shaped, upright form known as a **cartouche**. These remained popular into the second quarter of the c18, as did **architectural tablets** with columns or pilasters and a top pediment. As a rule, **segmental** and **broken** pediments were more common in the c17, triangular ones in the c18.

Broken pediment

Segmental pediment

By contrast, the variety of **materials** for the most prestigious monuments diminished after 1620, in favour of the strong contrasts offered by black, grey and white marble. These remained the usual choices until well into the c18, when there was a revival of interest in coloured marbles, especially in thin panels for backgrounds. By the end of the c18 the fashion had passed, and monochromes were back in vogue. Inexpensive, machine-cut marble slabs

Here lyeth the body of
Right Hon:ble THOMAS Earle
Viscount COLCHESTER & SAVAGE, of &
Baron DARCEY of CHICK who y°
the 1st day of September 16...
at his House in great Queen Street in
Parish of S:t GYLES in the FEILDS, in y°
County of MIDLESEX & was here Interr'd
the 14th day of October following
In the 67th year of his Age.

87. The monument to Earl Rivers at St Michael, Macclesfield,
Cheshire, of 1696. The gesturing figure and bold framing draperies are
typical of some larger types of English Baroque church monument

88. Detail of Thomas Scheemakers's monument to Mary Russell, 1787, at St Peter, Powick, Worcestershire. Here the mourning figure rests on top of a Neoclassical sarcophagus on which the deceased portrait appears in relief. The inscription is below

also saw off much of the demand for local stones for monuments by the early C19. **Bronze** was used for a few C17 busts and effigies, but never caught on for large-scale funerary sculpture.

The grandest monuments of the period after 1660 magnify the architectural elements into giant **Baroque**-style backdrops of columns and broken or open pediments like classical altar reredoses, frequently with big carved draperies. In front of these installations, the effigies may appear reclining or standing like figures on a stage, often gesturing as in life. The taste for **drapery** extended to tablets and cartouches, which may be enhanced with other small-scale sculpture, typically garlands, cherub-heads or skulls, as well as heraldry. The best of these cartouches are exquisitely carved, and comparable to the achievements of Grinling Gibbons in wood.

The **Neoclassical** taste of the mid C18 to early C19, which sought direct inspiration from classical Antiquity, ushered in a new range of forms. Flattened pyramids or obelisk shapes rather than reredos-type backdrops with columns came into favour. Mouldings and other architectural details became sparer and thinner, especially after 1760. Portraits were more often shown as busts on circular bases or as reliefs in profile, sometimes in Roman rather than contemporary dress. Larger monuments may supplement the portraits with graceful sculpted personifications of virtue or mourning, or with cherub attendants.

A budget version of this attendant-figure formula, represented thousands of times on tablets by sculptors ranging in ability from fashionable Royal Academicians to village masons, shows a draped figure mourning by a tomb, often with a weeping willow alongside. Skulls fell from favour after the mid C18, but other emblems of mortality appeared, such as extinguished torches and the very common depictions of sarcophagi or urns. By the early C19 some tablets were modelled directly on Roman or Greek funerary monuments, regardless of their pagan origins. More explicitly religious or moralizing subjects also found favour in the **Late Georgian** period, such as cut flowers (for those who died young), or guardian angels with or without a representation of the deceased.

Neo-Gothic monuments also appear in quantity around this time, at first usually rendered in classical lettering within an architectural frame. However, Victorian practice increasingly inclined to commemorate the dead by means of engraved brass plaques, stained glass, or the gift of furnishings. There was a revival of **figured brasses** in this period, especially for the clergy. Large **sculpted monuments** were nevertheless still erected here and there after 1840, in particular the revived form of tomb-chest with fully recumbent effigy. Victorian monuments of this class in parish churches usually continue existing dynastic sequences or commemorate wealthy donors, although cathedrals can show plenty of sculpted monuments to bishops and deans.

The **late C19 and early C20** witnessed a modest revival of smaller church monuments. Some of these drew on new fashions in small-scale bronze sculpture, with figurines or portrait medallions. Others explored the potential of mosaic and inlay, techniques in sympathy with the Arts and Crafts Movement. The early C20 revaluation of English classical architecture stimulated a revival of C17 tablet types, often beautifully lettered and sometimes close enough to the original to deceive all but a close inspection.

Post-war monuments are generally discreet. Many of the best take the form of lettered slabs in the Arts and Crafts tradition. **War memorials** from the Boer War and two world wars are another story, as they can be of all shapes and sizes, from run-of-the-mill nameboards supplied by joiners or monumental masons to ambitious church furnishings such as reredoses, side chapels and organs.

Another type of monument is the **hatchment**, a painted display of heraldry on a square ground set diamond-wise. These boards were displayed on the fronts of great houses when the owner died, before being consigned to the church. They frequently occur in groups from the same family, and date mostly from the C18 and C19.

Hatchments should not be confused with **royal arms**. Their display was required by law in every church after 1660, reversing the purge of such royal symbols during the republican Commonwealth. Most are painted on board or canvas, or carved in wood, but other media were used too: carved stone, moulded plaster, and a few castings in metal or the artificial compound known as Coade stone. The arms may display the year of making, or be datable less exactly by reign or heraldic period. By 1850 the convention was out of favour, and the relatively few royal arms that remain from Victoria's reign belong mostly to her first decade (i.e. 1837 onwards).

Benefaction boards record gifts to the parish, typically in the form of endowments or sums of money for regular distribution. They are often found at the W end, especially in the space under the tower.

▶ 89. Carved royal arms of James II (1685–8), from St Mary, West Malling, Kent

11 CHURCHES 1660–1840

The Restoration of King Charles II in 1660 also re-established the Church of England, with its hierarchy of bishops and its emphasis on dignity and ceremony in worship. Six years later, the Great Fire of London created a pressing need for new churches. Most of them were designed by Sir Christopher Wren (1632–1723), a brilliant polymathic architect already in the king's service, and his assistants. The concept of an architect's role as separate from that of the builder was still novel at this time: well into the C18, churches and other major buildings were routinely designed and built by master masons, bricklayers and other artisans. To complicate the picture, some gentlemen-amateurs also took up the practice of design, and the study of individual cases has shown too that designs supplied on paper by architects often left a great deal to the builders' initiative.

The influence of WREN nonetheless appears almost everywhere in church architecture of the later C17 and early C18. Unlike Inigo Jones at Covent Garden, Wren dispensed with classical porticoes, and provided the fifty-plus London churches produced by his office between c. 1670 and the mid 1690s with bell-towers of the traditional kind. Many of them had spires too, most of which were added later as funds allowed. But Wren also embraced plans without deep projecting chancels, creating interiors that were better suited to congregational Protestant worship. Another innovation was the extensive use of galleries, partly to accommodate those from neighbouring parishes whose burnt churches were not replaced. Some of these were fully integrated into the design, especially by the device of resting the galleries on the tall bases of columns that rose to support the roof. A few churches also adopted centralizing or cross-type plans, with a N–S axis as well as the familiar orientation from W to E.

The detailed motifs of these London churches were similarly diverse. Aisles had round-arched arcades or simple colonnades. Ceilings were flat, domed, barrel- or groin-vaulted, or multiple

90. Elevation drawings of some City church spires. Those still extant are (numbered from the left): top row, St Andrew Holborn (2), St Michael Paternoster Royal (5), Christ Church Newgate Street (6); bottom row, St Lawrence Jewry (1), St Edmund the King (2), St Mary Abchurch (3), St Mary Aldermary (5), St Dunstan-in-the-East (6)

combinations of these, with enrichments in the thickly modelled plasterwork of the time. Windows were round-headed, segment-headed, straight-headed, circular or half-circular, and often quite simply treated. Larger windows sometimes had stone mullions and transoms, and basic round-headed tracery within the main arch. Carved swags and garlands were used as external ornament. External angles were treated plainly or ornamented with QUOINS, with pilasters on the upper stages of some towers. Parapets were plain, moulded, balustraded, or pierced in any one of a dozen different patterns, with urns and obelisks by way of vertical interest. Steeples were of stone or leaded timber: some adopted traditional octagonal spire shapes, others consisted of obelisks, domes, cupolas, stepped pyramids, or even superimposed colonnades, often used in vertical combination. Here was an inexhaustible source of ideas and motifs for later generations of church builders, imitated directly or echoed at second hand.

The next great development also derived from London, where rapid urban growth encouraged the government to sponsor a fresh series of churches under an Act of 1710. These are more monumental than Wren's City churches. Most are wholly ashlar-faced, and stand free on all sides; Nicholas Hawksmoor's great East End trio of Christ Church, Spitalfields, St Anne, Limehouse, and St George-in-the-East belong to this class. In many cases the churches are governed externally by a GIANT ORDER (classical columns or pilasters that embrace the full height of a building, or more than one major storey within it). An extensive crypt or UNDERCROFT provided space for burials, which were then still common within the walls of churches.

The most influential church of this generation, as it happens not built under the 1710 Act, is St Martin-in-the-Fields in Westminster, of 1721–6 by James Gibbs. Here the full temple-type WEST PORTICO adopted by some of the post-1710 churches is combined with a fully developed stone steeple on the same axis, a treatment that was still current a hundred years later. St Martin's also avoids any suggestion of a cross-axis, unlike many of the 1710 generation.

▸ 91. Christ Church, Spitalfields, London, by Nicholas Hawksmoor, 1714–29

◁ 92. The neo-Gothic tower of Daniel Hague's St Paul, Portland Square, Bristol, 1789–94, is combined with a classical interior

▷ 93. The circular nave of St Chad, Shrewsbury, Shropshire, of 1790–2 by George Steuart, represents the experimental phase of Neoclassical church architecture

Not mentioned so far are the first churches of the GOTHIC REVIVAL. A handful of Wren's City churches belong to this class, with or without the incorporation of older parts that had survived the flames. St Mary's church in Warwick, also partly rebuilt in a contemporary version of Gothic after a fire of 1694, shows that some other architects were thinking along similar lines (in this case a local master builder, Sir William Wilson). Scattered instances of neo-Gothic occur among c18 churches too. These increasingly showed an interest in accurate imitation of detail, even if the general effect and the materials used (plaster vaulting, cast-iron tracery) are still thoroughly Georgian. Churches by provincial architects or master builders – a distinction not always exact even into the c19 – occasionally mix explicitly Gothic and classical details, as at St Paul, Bristol (1789–94).

A contrasting movement in church design, associated with the NEOCLASSICAL trend in architecture generally, was much less deferential to traditional ideas of what a church should look like.

Buildings of this class are few, wildly diverse, and always unforgettable; most belong to the last four decades of the c18. Newcastle upon Tyne and Shrewsbury have churches with oval or round naves, combined with multi-storey spires; Great Packington (Warwicks.) has a giant cross vault on simplified Doric columns inside, and a low, domed tower on each corner; Ayot St Lawrence (Herts.) is treated like a small classical temple with column-screens to either side, and no tower at all. As with church monuments, architectural decoration followed the trend towards thin, spare outlines and conventionalized rather than naturalistic forms, especially in plasterwork.

94. St Andrew, Kirkandrews-on-Esk, Cumberland (now Cumbria), 1775. A simple but architecturally refined Georgian village church, designer unknown

London apart, neither the late C17 nor the C18 was a great age for church building, and many counties have little to show from this time. Making new parishes was a complicated matter in legal terms, and newly populous districts were therefore often served instead by CHAPELS OF EASE, an expedient inherited from medieval times. PROPRIETARY CHAPELS were similarly built on private initiative, especially in urban areas, and rarely survive intact. Each was funded by its members' pew rents, like the simple chapels of the Nonconformists which they often resembled, but their services were those of the Church of England.

Likewise, when RURAL CHURCHES were rebuilt simple box-like forms were often employed, with no great architectural display outside or in. Decaying medieval chancels might be replaced with shorter versions in a basic classical style, regardless of what the nave looked like. Similarly, naves and chancels were rebuilt together as attachments to structurally sound medieval towers. Hybrid buildings like these were often taken in hand by Victorian improvers, either to rework the Georgian parts to look more medieval, or to replace them altogether. The same treatment was applied to churches in towns, where these had been modernized with classical frontispieces and other embellishments.

Georgian quiescence was vigorously reversed after 1818, the year in which Parliament once again endorsed state funding of new churches, this time across the whole of England and Wales. The grant for this purpose was administered by a separate commission, hence the term COMMISSIONERS' CHURCHES. A second Act in 1824 expanded the scheme. However, the size of individual grants steadily diminished into the 1840s as funds were spread more thinly around the rapidly urbanizing nation. Where local funding was in short supply, many of these new churches were cheap-looking and rather bleak outside and in.

Not all the churches built during this period were supported and vetted by the Commission, but they tend to share general similarities. Many of the first wave harked back to the London churches of the 1710 Act: architecturally grandiose buildings with bold w towers and classical porticoes, equipped internally with galleries round three sides, and conspicuously placed in urban or suburban areas. Several followed the fashionable GREEK REVIVAL, but other designs invoked the precedents of Wren and Gibbs, especially in their multi-storey steeples. Neo-Gothic designs appeared too, and after 1824 the Gothic quotient rapidly increased, squeezing out classical designs almost completely by 1830. Behind this movement lay a growing conviction that Gothic was the most appropriate and inspiring style for the Church of England, as well

as a sure means of maintaining a visible difference from the chapels of other denominations.

Unlike most Victorian churches, these Late Georgian designs tend to be rigidly symmetrical in plan. Classical or Gothic, they lack a deep projecting chancel (unless one has been added later). Gothic details of this period also have a stereotyped quality, repeating the same elements where a Victorian designer might introduce variety and incident. This applies whether the church is stone-faced or of brick with stone dressings. Another tell-tale in the case of stone churches is the use of equal courses of large ashlar blocks, where a medieval or Victorian church would employ smaller stones in courses of varying height. Stucco does not appear, the Commissioners having prohibited it as a facing material.

Regardless of style, this generation of churches abandoned the spatial adventures of the late C18 in favour of single oblong interiors, with or without aisles. Plans with a cross-axis also fell out of use. On the other hand, ceilings and roofs showed more variety. Some took the form of false vaults of timber and plaster, or plaster versions of the panelled, low-pitched roofs of the late Middle Ages; but by the 1830s it was also increasingly common to imitate medieval open timber roofs, at this stage usually in a rather thin and spindly way.

95. St Peter, Brighton, Sussex, 1824–8, by Sir Charles Barry. The strict symmetry and the use of well-observed Gothic details on an essentially Georgian design are typical of the Commissioners' churches of the 1820s. The two side doorways gave access to galleries over the aisles

PEWS, GALLERIES AND LIGHTING AFTER 1660

Most Georgian **pews** were in effect personal or family properties, secured by payment of pew rents to the parish. They were supplied with lockable doors, and commonly had tall sides for protection against draughts, hence the term **box pews**. Almost all urban churches, and a great many rural ones, had been reseated in this fashion by c. 1840.

Some box pews took the form of large enclosures with benches lining every side, so that a family could sit together. Other variants include the so-called **squire's pew**, an unusually grand and conspicuously placed enclosure for the most important family of the parish. **Free seats**, intended for the poor of the parish and for visitors from elsewhere, were customarily provided by means of open benches.

These arrangements were offensive to many Victorian reformers. The segregation of the poor from the rent-paying contradicted the claim that the Church of England was there for everyone, and the excessive amount of floor space taken up by many enclosed pews was problematic at a time when efforts were being made to increase seating capacity. To many eyes, box pews were also an incongruous presence in medieval and neo-Gothic church interiors. Most churches were therefore reseated with uniform open-ended pews, or free-standing **benches** (sometimes also, confusingly, called pews), and the rental system was gradually abolished. Sometimes the old pews were cut down and reused instead, for reasons of sentiment or economy.

Also removed after 1840 were most of the **galleries** that had been installed in a great many medieval churches and incorporated into the design of many new ones. These now survive best in the form of **west galleries**, often in conjunction with an organ (before the Victorian period, the w gallery was the traditional place for the church choir and any other musicians). Classical churches that have lost their N and S galleries may betray the former arrangement by a two-storey arrangement of windows along the sides, but in galleried neo-Gothic churches the windows were almost always made to run up unbroken across the gallery backs. Where a church retains a full complement of galleries, they are more likely to have kept their original seating than the main floor area.

▷ 96. Box pews in a Georgian church interior at St Mary, Avington, Hampshire, 1768–71. The pulpit, reredos, communion rails of wrought iron, brass chandelier, and hatchment (right) are all characteristic of the period

Some later Victorian churches, especially in towns, dispensed with fixed seating in favour of **chairs**. The inspiration was Continental, although the chairs – where the original ones survive – are commonly of the English type with rush seating. More recently, the number of churches equipped with movable chairs has been steadily increasing at the expense of pews of all types, as congregations seek greater flexibility of use.

A church that has retained its Georgian pews and galleries may also have one or more brass **chandeliers**. A few chandeliers or candelabra survive from before the Reformation, but most belong to the years between 1660 and c. 1820–30, when the advent of gas lighting (in towns) and the encroaching neo-medieval taste drove them from favour. The most familiar type has double-curved arms extending in one or more tiers from a spindle which ends in a large sphere or (later) an ornamented urn-like shape. Chandeliers were sometimes bestowed as gifts, and may bear a date and the name(s) of maker or donor.

Whether or not they had chandeliers, most churches were formerly equipped with **sconces** or candle-holders attached to the walls and pews, and also fixed on or near the pulpit. These survive best in rural churches that have never been modernized. The gas fittings of the C19 are now rarer, although some Victorian **gasoliers** have been successfully adapted for electricity. A few churches still use oil lamps, historically the intermediate technology between candles and gas.

CHURCH RESTORATION IN THE NINETEENTH CENTURY

The later story of all the fittings and furnishings so far described is bound up with the C19 movement to restore churches to something like an ideal medieval form. The movement can be traced back to scattered antiquarian initiatives in the C18, and to the growth in scholarly understanding of medieval architecture during the early C19. Around 1840 it emerged as a national force for the first time. Crucial to this movement were the architect A. W. N. Pugin (1812–52), a Catholic convert with a brilliant instinct for neo-medieval design in any medium, and the Ecclesiologists (alias the Cambridge Camden Society, formed in 1839), a vocal clique of young churchmen who identified medieval architecture and furnishings with religious regeneration. But the movement also drew strength from more widespread feelings, rooted in both nationalism and Romanticism. English Gothic architecture was increasingly revered as a precious but often neglected inheritance, and the Middle Ages were widely idealized on social and aesthetic grounds, sometimes as a critique of the failings of contemporary life.

97. The w front of St Mary, Nottingham, showing the classical frontage of 1762. In 1846–50 this was replaced by W.B. Moffatt to a Gothic design of c. 1400, in harmony with the rest of the nave

98. Interior of the c13 church of St Anthony, St Anthony-in-Roseland, Cornwall, as restored in 1850 by a clerical amateur, the Rev. C.W. Carlyon. The patterned tile floor, pulpit and other woodwork are all typical of advanced Gothic Revival work of the period

Church restorations sometimes happened in single campaigns, but in at least as many cases the work proceeded in phases, as funds allowed or as the need arose. Structural decay sometimes demanded attention, in which case the parish typically sought to carry out other improvements at the same time. The age-old division of responsibility for the building between parish and patron or rector also tended to complicate matters. In some parishes, different architects and contractors worked simultaneously on nave and chancel; sometimes the parish struggled in vain to get the patron to stump up; sometimes it was the other way round. Once the builders had departed, individual gifts enhanced the restored building with new fittings and furnishings, often evidenced by commemorative inscriptions.

However varied their timescales, most restorations shared similar aims. Ordinary neglect was reversed, making churches weather-tight and structurally sound. Typical remedies included making drainage ditches around the walls of churches that had been sinking into the damp earth of their churchyards. Floors were re-laid, especially in the chancel, using decorated tiles of neo-medieval design. Where they were not vigorously restored, furnishings in a medieval church might also be wholly or partly replaced with neo-medieval ones, especially seating and anything with classical details. Screens reappeared across chancel arches, and stalls for choirs were set up within the chancel, adapting cathedral practice for parish use. Galleries were mostly purged, and three-decker pulpits cut down or banished. Sometimes the old furnishings were re-set or reused: box pews might become wall panelling, or displaced Commandments boards might be set up under the tower. Tower spaces were also commonly used as a refuge for monuments that were considered obtrusive, especially in churches whose inner walls were stripped of their plaster. External walls were often stripped too.

The architectural programme likewise combined practical improvement with neo-medieval ideals. Where extra capacity was needed, aisles were added or naves and chancels rebuilt on a grander scale. Many churches acquired new vestries and organ chambers, especially where the organ was moved from a w gallery or aisle into the chancel. Any embellishments or alterations that belonged conspicuously to the post-medieval period were at risk, especially

where they arose from Georgian churchwardens' taste for neatness, uniformity or comfort (hat pegs and exposed stove-piping were among the restorers' targets).

Medieval features that had decayed were renewed, usually with the aim of matching the old work. Materials were another matter: restorers often used a different kind of stone from the original, especially the cheap, widely available and easily worked Bath stone. Other signs of restorers' work include sharp-edged and over-regular carved detail, and headstops with conventionalized Victorian features. But a good restoration architect also knew how to scan the fabric for evidence of lost medieval work, such as fragments of tracery or ornamented parapets, in order to re-create what had been lost. Similarly, where traces of defunct features such as blocked-up windows were exposed by stripping or re-plastering, they were commonly valued as historical evidence and left visible.

Even so, a great deal of new work was frankly speculative, and sometimes anachronistic or incongruous in terms of the building's true date and character. Not every architect who took an old church in hand was by any measure a scholar of medieval architecture. Fewer still were free to watch over the work in progress from day to day, and a great deal of evidence that might have emerged from the fabric or furnishings was inevitably destroyed without record. There was also a widespread tendency to push churches back to an imagined or inferred earlier form, so that a C13 transept with C15 windows and roof might be remodelled with replacements of the older type. This happened not only from a desire for consistency, but also because the Gothic of the Early English and Decorated periods was commonly held to represent the style at its purest. Conversely, Perpendicular was widely considered a debased and ill-proportioned style, especially in its later forms.

Not everyone was happy with these changes. Some simply disliked seeing so much alteration to buildings in which they had worshipped all their lives. Many educated Victorians, architects not excluded, also regarded Elizabethan and C17 work as both historically

▲   100. The C14 chancel screen at St John the Baptist, Lound, Suffolk, as restored with a new rood loft by Ninian Comper, 1913

interesting and aesthetically valid (although Georgian furnishings found fewer defenders).

The very concept of restoration also came under attack. The influential critic John Ruskin (1819–1900) protested that 'restored' work was nothing but a modern forgery. Gentler and less invasive forms of repair were pioneered by the Society for the Protection of Ancient Buildings, co-founded in 1877 by the artist-craftsman and social reformer William Morris (1834–96). A particular bugbear of the society was 'scrape', the habit of stripping interior plaster to show the rubble stone beneath. Churches that have been repaired according to the S.P.A.B.'s methods can often be recognized by little insertions of close-laid tiles, a material chosen in order to make a clear distinction between repairs and original work.

As Victorian repairs and insertions decay in their turn, it has become more common to return to the principle of matching repair, where possible using materials close to or identical with the original. More broadly, many Victorian church restorations can now be viewed in a more favourable light. They ensured that decaying buildings were rescued from collapse, and infused in many cases with imaginative and creative spirit. Much fine craftsmanship and embellishment was also introduced, not always at the expense of furnishings of comparable or superior quality.

◄ 101. Wall painting of the Tree of Jesse by Nathaniel Westlake, 1884, at the heavily restored Norman church of All Saints, East Garston, Berkshire

POST-MEDIEVAL STAINED GLASS

Except for later installations of imported work, there is little stained glass of the C17 and C18 in English parish churches. Limited revivals of the medium did occur during these years, notably in the 1610s–30s and intermittently in the C18, but the recipients were mostly cathedrals, college chapels and private houses. Renaissance pictorial conventions remained in force, and most glass of this period makes extensive and painterly use of bright enamels. C18 windows are frequently translations of works by leading painters of the time, rather than original compositions.

Encouraged by the early C19 fascination with the Middle Ages, a few artists were already producing stained glass in a medieval idiom by the end of the 1820s. The turning point in the revival followed in the 1840s. Among its central figures was the architect A. W. N. Pugin (*see also* p. 143), who employed a

102. Detail of the s aisle window of St Mary, Northill, Bedfordshire, of 1664

103. A.W.N. Pugin's w window at St Saviour, Leeds, c. 1845, executed by Michael O'Connor

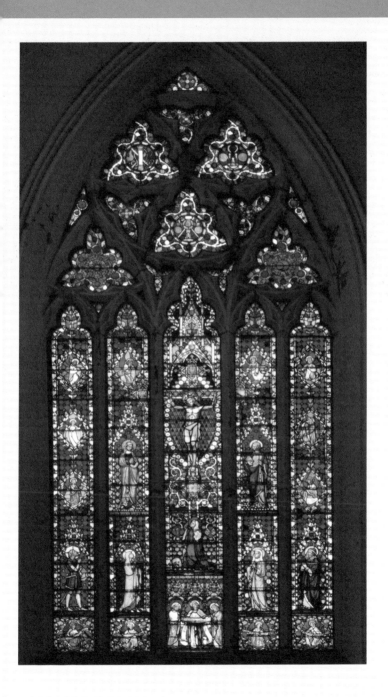

▲ 104. An aisle window made by Morris & Co. in 1876–7 for St Mark, New Ferry, Cheshire. The designer was Edward Burne-Jones

succession of makers in his quest to produce glass capable of matching the intense medieval colours. Most neo-medieval glass of the 1840s–50s looks back to the deep, bright hues and small figures of the C13–C14, but figures in Renaissance styles may be found too, often set within a Gothic surround.

By 1860 glass of medieval inspiration had diversified into bolder compositions and fiercer colours, in the hands of makers such as Clayton & Bell and William Morris's firm. Morris and his circle also sought to foster glass-making as a craft, as against the industrialized production emerging from big concerns such as Wailes & Co. of Newcastle. Many later Morris windows display the influential use of dark foliage as a background for figures, and the turn to Renaissance-type pictorialism for the figures themselves, especially those by the firm's leading designer Edward Burne-Jones. Other prolific makers active in the last third of the C19 include Burlison & Grylls and Charles Eamer Kempe, both of whom looked for inspiration to German and Flemish glass of c. 1500. Most Late Victorian and early C20 stained glass likewise depends on Late Gothic or Renaissance conventions, rather than close imitation of early medieval formulae.

Kempe's studios worked on a large scale, producing over 4,000 windows. The mature style is easily recognizable, with its combination of muted, dusty blue colouration, mild-featured figures, and repetitive canopy work. Other makers active around 1900 explored the practice of glass-making according to the Morris-inspired ideals of the Arts and Crafts Movement, in which design and execution were the work of a single master and his (or her) assistants. Christopher Whall and his pupil Mary Lowndes, later of Lowndes & Drury, were among the leading Arts and Crafts makers. Both used the distinctive and costly technique of slab glass, composed of thick and richly coloured pieces cut from the sides of vessels blown into square moulds. Pinks, purples and other non-medieval colours are typically juxtaposed in Arts and Crafts glass with strongly drawn, often near-monochrome faces and flesh. Stereotyped architectural surrounds are dispensed with.

Glass of all types from this period tends to be better made than early and mid-Victorian windows, which suffer quite often from fading or flaking. The loss of a Victorian window, whether because of decay, damage (including

▲ 105. Glass by Christopher Whall from St Saviour, Shanklin, Isle of Wight, c. 1913

154

wartime bomb blast) or distaste, is sometimes betrayed by the survival of tracery glazing, or by the presence of a brass inscription strip on the inner window sill. Some C19 windows may also have been replaced, having fallen victim to later Victorian or C20 changes in taste. This explains why an E window is sometimes decades later in date and style than those in the chancel side walls or nave, even though the common practice was to install stained glass in the E window first. Glass may also have been moved between windows, not always making a perfect fit, or have been subjected to the mid-C20 fashion for 'pickling', in which the figures and pictorial scenes from a dismembered Victorian window were re-set in new plain glass.

Late Gothic, Renaissance and Arts and Crafts styles all carried on after the 1920s. The historical styles show a steady loss of conviction, but Arts and Crafts traditions were refreshed by Modernist ideas of simplified draughtsmanship and intensified or non-naturalistic colours. New techniques also appeared. *Dalle-de-verre* glass, invented in France, uses a matrix of cement or resin to set small pieces of deeply coloured glass in mosaic-like patterns. It was most popular around 1960–70, especially for new churches. A more durable (and usually cheaper) fashion, and one better suited to historic buildings, involves the use of etching, engraving or sand-blasting on clear, coloured or frosted glass, to make images that may be figurative or abstract.

106. The E window of St Michael and All Angels, Marden, Kent, by Patrick Reyntiens, 1963. The subject is Christ in Majesty

13 VICTORIAN AND EDWARDIAN CHURCHES

Victorian churches are as plentiful as they are diverse. A total of 3,765 were built or rebuilt for the Church of England between 1835 and 1875 alone; in the peak decade of the 1860s new churches were consecrated at an average rate of just under two a week. Churches were planted in expanding suburbs, towns and resorts old and new; decayed or unfashionable rural churches were replaced; village settlements which had moved away from the site of their ancient churches were supplied with more conveniently located replacements. Some new churches came about because the existing one could no longer cope with the numbers wishing to attend. Other foundations were fostered by the knowledge that a grand new church would lend 'tone' and supply a social focus to new residential districts. Others

▲ 107. St Mary, Windermere, Westmorland (now Cumbria), 1847–8, by the Rev. J.A. Addison. Built as a proprietary chapel for a fast-growing resort, it was rapidly enlarged and converted to a parish church

108. Interior of St Margaret, Leiston, Suffolk, by E.B. Lamb, 1853–4. A good example of the Evangelical or Low Church plan-type, with shallow chancel and broad transepts. The bold roof structure is also unlike any medieval English model

still were built on the missionary principle, in the hope of attracting a congregation from the membership of Nonconformist chapels, or from those who did not attend worship at all. Some churches were built from a commemorative impulse, or out of religious devotion; many that were already planned or partly built benefited similarly from the new spirit of generosity and sacrifice, becoming grander and visually richer.

All this occurred without any direct government sponsorship on the model of the 1818 Act. Instead, local initiatives increasingly took command. Many dioceses had their own church-building societies, and bishops and other clergy proved adept at finding sites, donors and funds to carry on the work. One representative figure was the vicar of Bournemouth, the Rev. Alexander Morden Bennett, instrumental in founding or rebuilding eight churches in the growing resort during the 1850s–70s. Even after Bennett's death, yet another Bournemouth church was founded in his memory.

Ties between parish of residence and place of worship also weakened, especially in urban areas, and this encouraged the 'High' and 'Low' affiliations within the Church of England to provide new buildings shaped according to their differing expectations. In Bournemouth, those who did not approve of Bennett's High Churchmanship came together to build a church in which a more Evangelical, gospel-centred interpretation of the Anglican creed was proclaimed. Churches of this kind can often be distinguished by their plans: emphatic transepts, so that more of the congregation could sit directly facing the pulpit in the crossing, and a relatively shallow chancel.

All this is to say nothing of style, yet this is often the first aspect of a Victorian church that strikes the viewer. A rough narrative of how the different styles were used may be helpful here.

The 1840s were dominated by the ideal of a return to medieval English forms, often used with scholarship and conviction. The dominant figures in this very vocal movement, Pugin and the Ecclesiologists, have already been encountered in the context of church restoration, and the Ecclesiologists in particular drew no distinction in importance between restoration and new building. Earlier neo-Gothic churches tended to 'quote' individual motifs as elements of a whole that still owed much to Georgian models of symmetry and planning, but the new wave favoured deep chancels of medieval outline, and relished the picturesque compositions that could be achieved by providing a single aisle or placing a tower off-centre. Individual motifs such as windows were now also more likely to be adapted from those of comparably modest medieval buildings, rather than scaled down from a cathedral or abbey. Among the characteristic products of the 1840s that resulted was the unassuming little rural church with its bellcote and lancet or two-light windows, built of rubble stone.

Near-replicas of admired C13 and C14 English churches continued to appear well into the second half of the C19. A number of NEO-NORMAN churches were also built, especially in the 1840s. A handful of churches adopted a less imitative quasi-Romanesque style influenced by recent Continental work, sometimes called RUNDBOGENSTIL (German for 'round-arched style').

▲ 109. St Lawrence, Tubney, Oxfordshire (formerly Berkshire), 1845–7. One
of a handful of Anglican churches designed by A.W.N. Pugin, here using a
simple Dec style appropriate to a village place of worship

Then, after 1850, the creative impulse within the Gothic Revival
led to an unprecedented interest in Continental architecture as a
possible source for imitation. The reasons for this shift are complex. One factor was the growing realization that surviving English
medieval churches offered few prototypes for building on compact
urban sites (on which more below). Much impetus also came from
the conviction of many partisans of Gothic that it should be adapted
into a universal architectural language, capable of giving form and
expression to modern building types such as law courts and railway
stations. That meant looking abroad for possible models, especially

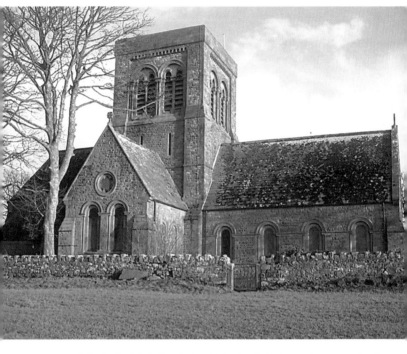

▲ 110. St Bride, Bridekirk, Cumberland (Cumbria), 1868–70, a late example of a neo-Norman church

▶ 111. Structural polychromy in the interior of William Butterfield's St Laurence, Alvechurch, Worcestershire, 1857–61

to the cities of Italy and northern Europe. Here was an inexhaustible supply of ideas and discoveries, including the bold combination by Italian architects of different materials to achieve effects of pattern, emphasis and expression – so-called structural polychromy. Brick, which had been despised as a late-coming and inferior material within the English Gothic story, suddenly became acceptable and even admirable after 1850.

Structural polychromy chimed in with the contemporary interest in geology. Ruskin drew a parallel between the strata of rock formations and the layered treatment of different materials in some

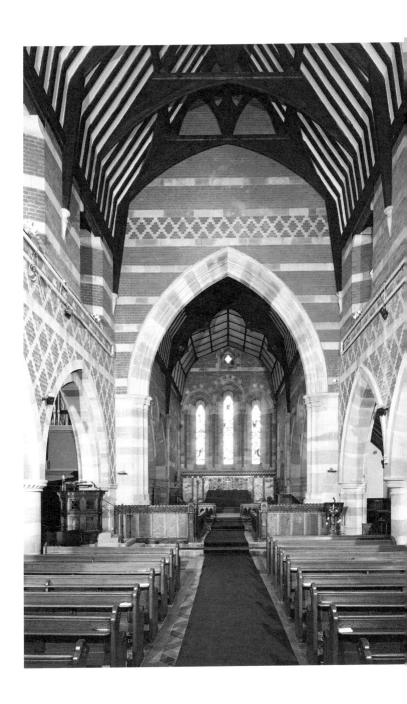

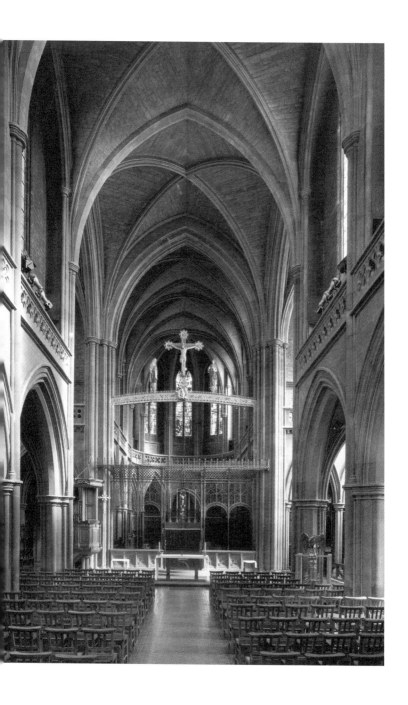

Italian medieval buildings. Brick also allowed the easy production of other types of pattern, such as diapering and chequering. The walls of many Victorian churches thus have a visual interest that is both distinct from, and intimately related to, the three-dimensional presence of windows, buttresses and other structural elements. Even churches that are faced largely or wholly in a single material may prove to be boldly polychromatic inside, where patterned brick walls and polished granite arcade shafts come into play.

More broadly, forms that would have been rejected by scholarly critics of the 1840s as un-English now acquired prestige and power from their Continental origins. France was one popular source, especially in the 1860s. Distinctively French features that were widely taken up in those years include tall, semicircular chancel apses, and big plate-traceried windows inspired by those from the infancy of Gothic in the late C12. Some of the most compelling exercises in the French manner were designed by John Loughborough Pearson (1817–97), whose churches often feature load-bearing vaults of brick or stone. The big crocket-type capitals associated with French Gothic were another opportunity for a display of the sort of carving especially in tune with mid-Victorian taste, which drew on both medieval conventions and the direct study of natural forms. A common point of reference for the latter, inevitably, was the naturalistic period of English Decorated carving (*see* p. 64).

Not every Victorian church that uses Continental motifs can be pigeonholed by period style or national school. Motifs and details from abroad, especially from France, were often combined with English ones, as in many churches by Sir George Gilbert Scott (1811–78), the most prolific and versatile of all Victorian architects. A good example is the use of cross-gables over the side windows, giving an up-and-down rhythm to the aisles. Other architects strove to develop a more comprehensively original style, while also evoking and honouring the medieval past. Bold polychromatic patterns and blunt, powerful forms derived only loosely from medieval

112. Interior of St Alban, Bordesley, Birmingham, 1879–81. One of J. L. Pearson's vaulted churches, showing strong French influence

precedent constituted an aesthetic in their own right for architects such as William Butterfield (1814–1900) and George Edmund Street (1824–81), to name but two.

Later Victorian churches in most cases owe less to this weighty, slab-sided manner. Architectural taste in general shifted towards lighter and more delicate forms, and younger church architects once again took up English models. This time the favoured period was not the c13 and early c14 Gothic beloved of the 1840s, but the late Decorated style as it began to move into the Perpendicular period. Pioneering churches in this new fashion include St John the Baptist, Tue Brook (Liverpool), of 1867–70, by George Frederick Bodley (1827–1907). Bodley was at once the most important architect to turn back to English Gothic and a hugely influential designer of furnishings and decorative schemes in his own right, including the use of damask-like patterns and stencilling for internal walls.

A similar aesthetic richness and concern for harmonious overall effect mark the churches of many architects under Bodley's influence, such as those of the Lancaster-based partnership of Edward Paley and Hubert Austin. In the 1870s Paley and Austin were among the first architects to push the revival of English Gothic forward into explicitly Perpendicular forms, and by 1900 churches wholly in the style of the English c15 were commonplace. By c. 1890 other architects were moving away from the commitment to archaeological exactitude, and pioneering buildings such as J. D. Sedding's Holy Trinity, Sloane Street, London (1888–90), have been aptly described as 'Free Gothic', even though the point of departure is still recognizably English.

All this is to say nothing of developments in planning and arrangement. Pugin's generation tended to conceive of their buildings as free-standing objects, regardless of whether they were to stand in isolation or fit into a denser urban setting. The first Anglican church

113. St John the Baptist, Tue Brook, Liverpool, 1867–70. An early example of G.F. Bodley's revival of c14 English forms, with furnishings by the architect. The rich decoration in Bodley's late style was designed by his former partner H.T. Hare, 1910 (restored with variations, 1968–71)

since Wren's time to demonstrate convincingly how this might be achieved was Butterfield's showpiece, All Saints, Margaret Street, in Marylebone, London, of 1849–59. Here the entrance is made via a small forecourt, formed by auxiliary buildings for use by the clergy and parish that are directly attached to the church itself. Remarkably, there are no windows at all in the N and E walls of the church, which demonstrates inside and out the potential of structural polychromy to dramatize and energize the outlines of the composition. These owe much to north German architecture, the slim spire especially. All Saints thus fused three mid-Victorian trends in one epoch-mak-

▲   115. St Bartholomew, Brighton, Sussex, 1872–4, by Edward Scott. An extreme instance of the mid-Victorian type of urban church, rising high above the surrounding houses. The style is early French Gothic, loosely interpreted; an intended chancel was never built

◄   114. The Perpendicular revival, represented by Hubert Austin's St George, Stockport, Cheshire, of 1891–8

ing design: the compact urban plan, the leap into polychromy, and the quest for Continental models.

By the late C19 a distinctive form had been adopted for many big urban churches, in which a single tall roof extended from w to e without the traditional drop in height for the chancel. Instead, the roofline was often broken by a bellcote at the division between nave and chancel, or a slim French-style spirelet of the type known as a FLÈCHE. Churches of this type thus dispensed with a deep chancel, chancel arch and screen on the medieval model, in favour of improved sight-lines between the congregation and the altar.

For similar reasons, separately expressed chancels of the period tend to be much less deep than in medieval times, and the chancel arch much wider. The setting of the altar was often enhanced by placing it in a polygonal or rounded apse, on the Continental model. Especially in a High Church parish, the altar might also be raised high up on a progression of steps, and the screen omitted in favour of a low wall at the chancel entrance. The ultimate model for plans of this type lay abroad, in the churches built after the Reformation in areas that had remained Catholic. The aim – to make the ritual at the altar more visible to the congregation – was identical in both cases.

A related change affected many churches with aisles, which were reduced in width and lost their seating altogether. All the congregation thus sat in the broad central vessel of the nave, in full view of the chancel. Churches with passage aisles of this kind often convey a powerful sense of spatial unity, especially when the roof soars high above. The effect may be concentrated still further where the aisles are formed not by true arcades but by openings pierced through short transverse lengths of wall. These cross-walls perform the structural function of buttresses placed within, rather than outside, the space enclosed by the outer walls. Aisles for free circulation were especially useful in churches where communion was frequent, so again there is a connection with High Church practices, although not an exclusive one.

In counterpoint to this drive towards unity, Late Victorian architects developed lesser spaces within the church in new ways. Instead of a side porch, the main entrance was sometimes made through a NARTHEX or transitional space at the w end. This typically appears as a low, lean-to attachment below the gabled end and w window of the nave proper. A separate enclosure off the w end of the nave might be provided for a BAPTISTERY, where christenings at the font could be performed away from the main interior. Separate chapels were also provided, reflecting the diversity of rituals embraced especially by High Church congregations, and these might be expressed as wider spaces at the ends of the aisles. By the late C19 some Anglican churches included a Lady Chapel, something that would have unthinkable a few generations before. In addition, certain churches followed the lead of All Saints, Margaret Street, in

▲ 116. Interior of St Augustine, Pendlebury, Manchester, 1871–4, depicted in G.F. Bodley's own watercolour. Another early and influential church by the architect, showing the use of passage aisles

attaching the accommodation for the clergy to the main building, and sometimes schools too.

The greater provision for clergy reflected the social mission of the Church of England. Schools, Sunday Schools, institutes, and lay societies and guilds of every kind proliferated during the C19 and into the C20, amidst lively debates as to how the Church should best

THE BUILDING NEWS, JAN 2 1880

117. The engraved design for William Emerson's St Mary, Brighton, Sussex, 1877–9, showing a powerful tower of which no more than the ground stage was built. The w end is bowed outwards to form a baptistery

spend its resources. These activities in turn help to explain the number of unfinished churches from the same period. The most common omission is a tower, often present only as a stump containing a porch. Where a tower is present to full height, it may still lack the intended spire. Sometimes the plan, whether fulfilled or not, was to build the nave in two or more phases, so that the w end is finished with what was meant to be a temporary wall, or with a continuation in a later and different style.

Another expedient was to put up a temporary or mixed-use building as a mission church. By the late c19 it was possible to order prefabricated church buildings of corrugated iron, and some of these so-called tin tabernacles remain in use today. The school-chapel combined both functions in a single building, usually with sliding screens to mark off the teaching space when not in use for worship.

The late C19 fashion for church halls offered another option, for the hall could be used for services while funds were raised to erect a proper church nearby. Where this never happened, or where the church was built but then given up, the hall may still be in use for worship.

The interiors of many Victorian churches of all types can similarly be thought of as incomplete works in progress, offering plenty

▲ 118. G.E. Street's St John, Howsham, East Yorkshire (formerly East Riding), 1859–60. An estate church that is also an example of the radically original forms embraced by some Gothic Revival architects

of spaces and surfaces for further enhancement. Even where money was available to complete the architect's design in full, a new church was often consecrated with only plain and basic furnishings in place, and gradually filled with better ones as funds and donations allowed. Many chancels display incomplete decorative schemes; few churches ever achieved a full complement of stained glass. Plain or patterned windows thus remain abundant, especially in clerestories and aisles.

A contrasting but much rarer type is the so-called estate church. These were typically private benefactions by pious squires or landlords, replacing or supplementing existing churches on their domains. In its fullest expression, an estate church was supplied from the outset with furnishings and decoration complete. Examples include the sequence built in the East Riding of Yorkshire by Sir Tatton Sykes with G. E. Street as architect, including Howsham and Garton-in-the-Wolds. Most churches of this kind date from before the mid 1870s, when the decline in the value and profitability of country estates increasingly made itself felt. New rural churches of the later C19 and C20 are more likely to have been paid for by incoming landlords enriched by industry or commerce.

Rural parish churches of any period are mostly unmistakable as such, but it can be more of a challenge to distinguish urban Anglican churches from those of Roman Catholics and Nonconformists, at least externally. One reason is the widespread adoption of Gothic after *c*. 1840 for non-Anglican places of worship, which also began to embrace towers and spires. Architects of Catholic churches shared the enthusiasm for churches of the type with a tall nave and shallow chancel. Where a church has passed into secular use, or has been taken over by a different denomination, its original affiliation can be still harder to tell. There may be a clue in the orientation, as the Church of England alone remained faithful to the medieval rule by which a church should have its altar at the E end.

▶   119. Interior of St Mary the Baum, Rochdale, Lancashire, an enlargement of 1909–11 by Ninian Comper of a small C18 church (left). The woodwork of the screen includes a few Renaissance details, suggestive of English work on the eve of the Reformation

120. St Edward the Confessor, Kempley Gloucestershire, 1902–3, by
A. Randall Wells. A strong church-like character achieved without direct
emulation of historic forms. The relief over the doorway was carved partly
by the architect himself

Although Edwardian churches do not constitute a separate type,
several late Victorian trends became more prominent in the decade
and a half after 1900. Free Gothic continued to make progress, and
late English Gothic also remained popular. The setting of the altar
remained a subject of near-obsessive interest for many. Some architects and churchmen devoted themselves to the scholarly investiga-
tion of late medieval practices, expressed in a mini-revival of screens
and in the popularity of the so-called 'English altar': a three-sided

enclosure of cloth hangings supported on wooden uprights known as riddel posts, which often have carved angels on top.

Other new churches bore witness to a weakening of the idea that Gothic was the best expression of Anglican identity. Alternative styles tried out here and there included neo-Byzantine and even classical. These remained exceptional before 1914, partly no doubt because both styles were already associated in England with the Roman Catholic Church. A more distinctively Anglican approach was pioneered by Sir Ninian Comper (1864–1960), who began to combine classical and English Gothic elements in a single building, as at his St Mary, Wellingborough (Northants), begun in 1908.

A special interest attaches to the handful of Anglican churches built according to ARTS AND CRAFTS tenets. This movement was in part a reaction against the dominance of historical styles, and many Arts and Crafts designers thought instead in terms of 'character'. The churches that resulted tend to be Gothic only in general outline and a few simple and evocative details, relying for effect on powerful massing and a frank display of their means and materials of construction. Celebrated examples from the 1900s include E. S. Prior's church at Roker, Sunderland, W. R. Lethaby's at Brockhampton, Herefordshire, and Randall Wells's at Kempley, Gloucestershire; the first two of these make use of mass concrete, and are roofed by means of transverse stone arches across the nave.

Such buildings remained wholly exceptional, but Arts and Crafts principles asserted themselves more widely in the design of count-less fittings and furnishings, including stained glass (*see* p. 153). The long afterglow of the Arts and Crafts Movement can be detected in church architecture and design well into the mid C20.

Most churches designed after the First World War are easily distinguished from those of the generations before. Building costs, already rising steeply in the years before 1914, were higher still when peace returned. Yet the demand for new churches held steady, especially for new suburbs and for the first giant council estates, so that new Anglican churches were consecrated at an average rate of one a month between the wars. The architecture that resulted tended to be leaner and sparer than that of the Edwardian years, and less dependent on costly displays of detail from historical styles. Although a bell-tower of some sort remained a common Anglican denominator, grand towers with spires were much less often attempted, and more churches were designed from the outset with spirelets or bellcotes only. Architectural mouldings and details were commonly stylized or simplified, and churches depended more for effect on unadorned walls. Phased construction was another useful expedient, and the

◄ 121. Detail of the W front of St Andrew, Ilford, London, 1923–4, by Sir Herbert Baker. A brick-built church in a simplified round-arched style, which makes extensive use of figurative decoration; here, a statuette by Sir Charles Wheeler

▲ 122. Diaphragm arches in the nave of St Mary, Pype Hayes, Birmingham, by Edwin F. Reynolds, 1929–30

Victorian convention that a church should not be consecrated until its chancel was complete was now less strictly enforced. Mission churches and parish halls continued to be provided as starting points for many new parishes.

The styles employed were also much more diverse than in Edwardian times. Round-arched designs proliferated, deriving more or less directly from Romanesque or Byzantine architecture, and weakening still further the age-old association between Gothic pointed arch and Church of England. Classical designs also became more common, although still scarce by comparison.

Increasing use was made of framed construction in the inter-war period, usually of reinforced concrete rather than steel. This was concealed in most cases by brick cladding, but might be expressed internally as a series of diaphragm arches along the nave. The same device was also still current for churches built of traditional load-bearing walls, a combination first introduced in mid-Victorian times. Plaster barrel vaults, flat timber ceilings and exposed, una-dorned roof trusses were also adopted.

interiors of this period are often whitewashed or plastered over, allowing the liturgical points of focus at the altar and pulpit to stand out against a neutral ground. This fashion for cool, whitened inte-riors can be traced back to a few Edwardian pioneers, notably the

▲ 123. St Martin, Ettinghall, Wolverhampton, by Lavender & Twentyman, 1938–9. A simplified round-arched design, conceived integrally with the vicarage, right

124. St Barnabas, Tuffley, Gloucester, by N. F. Cachemaille-Day, 1938–40

London vicar the Rev. Percy Dearmer; its rapid spread reflects a widely shared cultural reaction against anything with too strong a Victorian flavour. Muted shades and pale limed oak, rather than deep-hued stencilling and dark varnished wood, make up the characteristic palette of the inter-war church interior.

Another aspect of this post-Victorian mood was the embrace of Continental Baroque by one faction within the High Church wing. The trend was fostered by the Society of St Peter and St Paul, and was confined largely to furnishings; it is associated especially with the artist and designer Martin Travers (1886–1948). Painted statues of the Madonna, elaborate reredoses bedecked with candlesticks (rather than the two candles of Anglican tradition), and even gilded reliquaries acquired from the Continent began to appear where this fashion was taken up.

▲ 125. St Michael and All Angels, Hull, East Yorkshire (formerly East Riding), by Francis Johnston, 1957–8, fuses Neo-Georgian and Scandinavian motifs in a church of traditional outline and plan

By the 1930s the influence of the MODERN MOVEMENT had begun to pull church design further towards simplicity and abstraction. To younger architects such as N. F. Cachemaille-Day (1896–1976), the most influential models were Protestant and north European, from Holland, north Germany and Sweden. Plain brick, flat roofs, and blockish, square-topped forms are characteristic of these churches, many of which feature tall, slim windows with straight heads instead of arches. Any ornamental motifs are often rectilinear too, especially simple stepping or fluting of the brickwork.

Occasionally the traditional linear plan was also set aside. At Cachemaille-Day's St Michael and All Angels' church in Wythenshawe, Manchester, 1937, the altar is set transversely in one projection of an eight-pointed, star-shaped plan achieved by means of concrete framing. Less drastic departures from tradition included a handful of churches in which the altar was brought forward from the E end, so that it could stand closer to the congregation. In these cases the choir might also be relocated to a w gallery in the Georgian way, as at Ninian Comper's St Philip, Cosham (Portsmouth; 1936–8), where the altar stands beneath a BALDACCHINO or architectural canopy.

Post-war church architecture includes the selective restoration of bomb-damaged buildings, including many of Wren's in the City of London, in which the shortcomings of mid-century craftsmanship and budgets are sometimes all too apparent. Such projects could at

▲   126. Interior of St Paul, Bow Common, London, by Maguire & Murray, 1956–60. Modernist forms and materials are used in this centrally planned church, which features a free-standing altar under a baldacchino

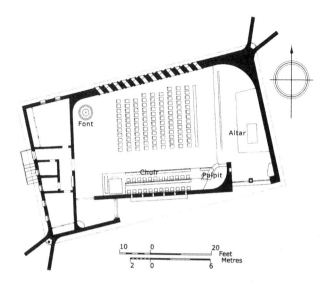

Font

Altar

Choir

Pulpit

10   0   20
                    Feet
                  Metres
  2   0   6

▲   127. The plan of St David, Beeston, Leeds, 1960–1, illustrates the inno-
vative arrangements adopted for many 1960s churches. The architect
was Geoffrey Davy of Kitson, Parish, Ledgard & Pyman

▶   128. St Paul, Haringey, London, by Peter Jenkins of Inskip & Jenkins,
1988–93. A church with a traditional linear plan, expressed in bold
elemental forms that evoke the idea of a church without following any
historical model

least draw on the official compensation fund for war damage, an
option not available to the new churches of the 1950s. These are
usually spartan at best, and can often seem both bland and unim-
aginative, like a watered-down overflow from the already mild
architectural currents of twenty years before, but in the hands of
a few exceptional architects the results are sometimes convincing.
Another trend carried over from the inter-war period was the inte-
gration of social functions such as halls and meeting rooms in a single complex, usually in a rather matter-of-fact way.

    Church buildings of the 1960s onwards present a livelier picture,
as the Liturgical Movement rapidly transformed ideas of planning

and use. The movement was international in scope, and its consequences were at least as radical for Roman Catholicism as for the Church of England. One of its central ideals was that worshippers should be brought closer to the altar so that communion could be celebrated in their midst, enhancing the sense of participation. Traditional linear plans were therefore set aside in favour of a variety of centralized or compact ones, in which altar, pulpit and font could be placed in dynamic or suggestive relationships. Architects also drew inspiration from a vast corpus of recent architecture on the Continent; in Germany alone, an estimated 8,000 churches had been built or restored by 1960.

The best examples of this generation broke drastically with tradition, but were animated by an unmistakably church-like spirit. The basic form is usually a brick box, with a plan that may be square, polygonal, partly curved, or some combination of these shapes. Roofs may be tilted, curved in a paraboloid profile, or of split pitch (to allow a glazed slot for lighting). The dramatic potential of natural light is also exploited by slot-like windows, high continuous clerestories or all-glass sections of wall. The altar may be free-standing near the centre, or placed in one corner so that the seating can make a fan-like arrangement around it, thus preventing the break-up of the congregation into separate blocks. Vertical interest may be lent to the exterior by slim spikes or spirelets, or by a free-standing concrete bell-tower in which the bells are sometimes visibly exposed. Similar forms were adopted for many Roman Catholic churches, of which the best-known example nationally is Frederick Gibberd's circular-plan cathedral at Liverpool (1962–7). Church art, a key feature of the design at Liverpool, may also be confidently represented in parish churches of this date, especially murals and stained glass of a Modernist character (*see* p. 155).

Buildings of this kind represent the last great high point of monumental church architecture in England. The succeeding fashion of multi-purpose buildings has done much to erode any sense of the church as a unique space. Dispensing with separate church halls, these interiors are arranged so that the main area can readily be cleared for meetings, performances and other community uses. An early and influential example was Martin Purdy's church of St Philip

▲ 129. Stained glass by Peter Strong from St Luke, Millom, Cumbria
(formerly Cumberland), 2002. Like much modern church glass its
imagery is commemorative rather than religious, here representing
one of the miners of the town

and St James at Hodge Hill, Birmingham (1963–8), which was initially kept open and in use for up to fourteen hours a day. Its sanctuary alone was reserved for exclusive religious use; the rest of the

▲ 130. St Thomas, East Shefford, Berkshire. An unrestored medieval church
from a vanished village, now in the care of the Churches Conservation Trust

interior was provided with sliding screens, to create smaller spaces according to need.

Hodge Hill's experimental church no longer exists: deemed too expensive to repair, it was demolished after closure in 2008. The parish now shares the local Congregationalist (United Reformed) church, a type of partnership that is becoming increasingly common as congregations decline. Likewise, new churches (or 'church centres') are now often designed for shared use by several denominations, and are therefore not shaped by distinctive Anglican traditions.

Churches in the early C21 are in turn subject to many pressures for physical change. Many parishes no longer follow the historic liturgy of the Church of England, and may have little or no use for the combination of fittings developed by the Victorians in a spirit of Anglican admiration for the Middle Ages. Other parishes may uphold these traditions, but seek to combine them with more flexible uses of the building. reordering, as the process is known, can therefore embrace anything between a modest reduction in the area taken up by pews and the near-total expulsion of existing fittings in order to create a multi-purpose space.

The broadening social use of churches also demands facilities such as meeting rooms, kitchens and lavatories, and these may be provided in new extensions or by subdividing and enclosing the main interior space (usually at the w end). Where skilful design, sensitive craftsmanship and good materials are brought to bear, insertions of this kind may actually enhance the interest of a church. This is a tall order, however, and in many more cases the new works may displace, damage or conceal older features and fittings, to the distress of those who love historic churches. The picture is more cheerful where furnishings are concerned, as good work continues to appear in many media, especially joinery and stained glass. More drastically, churches may embrace secular functions such as Post Offices, cafés or village shops – essential measures for widening use in the longer term, perhaps, but difficult to square with a suitable aesthetic approach inside the building.

Other churches are now effectively frozen in time, having been taken out of regular parochial use and transferred for preservation to bodies such as the Churches Conservation Trust and the Friends of Friendless Churches. Whatever changes the future may bring to the remainder, these buildings will remain intact as witnesses to the beauty, variety, and evocative power of the English parish church.

FURTHER READING

Books on churches fall into two classes, those dealing with buildings by county or area and those which explore individual periods or themes.

The most comprehensive COVERAGE BY AREA is in the *Buildings of England* series of the Pevsner Architectural Guides. These include notable fittings, furnishings and monuments with the building descriptions. Good detailed coverage can also be found in the ongoing *Victoria County History* series founded in 1899, especially more recent volumes, and in the county survey volumes of the former Royal Commission on Historical Monuments (England), although these extend across a smaller proportion of the country.

INDIVIDUAL ACCOUNTS on the National Heritage List issued by the DCMS vary hugely in quality, but the best are very good (www.historic-england.org.uk/listing/the-list). Of personal surveys, Simon Jenkins, *England's Thousand Best Churches* (1999) and Alec Clifton-Taylor, *English Parish Churches as Works of Art* (2nd edn, 1986) stand out. Clifton-Taylor's *The Pattern of English Building* (1987 edn) remains the best introduction to BUILDING MATERIALS. For relevant ARCHITECTURAL TERMS see *Pevsner's Architectural Glossary* (2010; also available as an app), and several C19 books by J.H. Parker reissued in facsimile.

Well-illustrated GENERAL STUDIES of church architecture include Pamela Cunnington, *How Old is that Church?* (1990) and Mark Child, *English Church Architecture: A Visual Guide* (1982). Jon Cannon, *Medieval Church Architecture* (Shire Books, 2014) covers greater churches as well as the parishes.

STUDIES BY PERIOD include surveys by Eric Fernie (1980) and H.M. and J. Taylor (1965–78) on Anglo-Saxon, a major study by Fernie (2000) on Norman, books by Jean Bony (1979), Nicola Coldstream (1994) and Paul Binski (2014) on aspects of Decorated, and John Harvey (1978) on Perpendicular. Warwick Rodwell, *The Archaeology of Churches* (2005) covers the whole medieval period.

Valuable accounts of the POST-REFORMATION CHURCH include Nigel Yates, *Buildings, Faith and Worship* (2nd edn, 2001), Terry Friedman, *The Eighteenth-century Church in Britain* (2011), Andrew Saint and Chris Brooks (eds), *The Victorian Church: Architecture and Society* (1995), and *The Twentieth Century Church* (*Twentieth Century Society Journal* 3, 1998).

Chris Webster and John Elliott (eds), *A Church as it Should Be* (2000), deals with the Ecclesiological Society, Michael Port, *Six Hundred New Churches* (2nd edn, 2006) with the wave of church building immediately before. Chris Brooks, *The Gothic Revival* (1999) is the best single-volume study of that subject. Individual unrestored churches are portrayed in Mark Chatfield, *Churches the Victorians Forgot* (2nd edn, 1987). Peter Howell and Ian Sutton (eds), *The Faber Guide to Victorian Churches* (1989) is a useful anthology of over 600 short descriptions.

ARCHITECTS of churches of the C17 to early C19 are covered in Howard Colvin, *A Biographical Dictionary of British Architects* (4th edn, 2008), medieval craftsmen in John Harvey, *English Medieval Architects* (2nd edn, 1984). Biographies of individual Victorian architects that shed a wider light on their times include Rosemary Hill, *God's Architect: Pugin and the Building of Romantic Britain* (2007) and Michael Hall, *George Frederick Bodley* (2014).

For a good general account of FURNISHINGS see Gerald Randall, *Church Furnishing and Decoration* (1980). More detailed studies are often old and hard to find, such as the early C20 sequence by Francis Bond covering woodcarvings, screens and fonts. Trevor Cooper and Sarah Brown, *Pews, Benches and Chairs* (Ecclesiological Society, 2011) brings together recent specialist scholarship.

England's medieval STAINED GLASS is being published in monographs and area studies by the Corpus Vitrearum Medii Aevi. General accounts of later periods include Martin Harrison, *Victorian Stained Glass* (1980), Peter Cormack, *Arts & Crafts Stained Glass* (2015), and Mark Angus, *Modern Stained Glass in British Churches* (1985).

For detailed information on BRASSES, there is nothing to match the county surveys produced by the Monumental Brass Society. Issued alphabetically, the books have so far reached *Huntingdonshire* (2012). Sally Badham and Martin Stuchfield, *Monumental Brasses* (Shire Books, 2009) covers all areas. David Meara's *Victorian Monumental Brasses* (1983) and *Modern Memorial Brasses* (1996) deal with recent centuries.

For MONUMENTS, Brian Kemp, *English Church Monuments* (1980) is the best one-volume survey, and the same author's paperback for Shire Books is useful too. The lives and works of individual sculptors from later centuries are summarized in Ingrid Roscoe, *A Biographical Dictionary of Sculptors in Britain, 1660–1851* (2009).

INDEX OF TERMS

Illustrations are indicated by italic page numbers.

ILLUSTRATION SOURCES AND CREDITS